T0385562

Native Provenance

Native Provenance
The Betrayal of Cultural Creativity

GERALD VIZENOR

University of Nebraska Press | LINCOLN

[CONTENTS]

Native Provenance

[1]

Gossip Theory

Native Irony and the Betrayal of Earthdivers

Native American Indians and Jews are the unmissable monitors of gossip theory, sorts of separatism, and cultural survivance. Natives were once boldly nominated in churchy hearsay as the descendants of the Lost Tribes of Israel. Jews and natives were revealed as an ancestral union of tradition and torment, removal and murder, the outsiders in colonial discoveries, crusades, and crude missions of Christianity.

Thomas Thorowgood proclaimed in *Jewes in America, or Probabilities That the Americans Are Jewes* that the "Indians do themselves relate things of their Ancestors, suteable to what we read of the Jewes in the Bible, and elsewhere. . . . The rites, fashions, ceremonies, and opinions of the Americans are in many ways agreeable to the custome of the Jewes, not onely prophane and common usages, but such as be called solemn and sacred."[1]

Hallelujah for the suitable and the sacred, and three centuries later the disparate gossip theory of a spiritual and cultural union continues, but with a greater potentiality for survivance stories and a sense of ancestral unintended irony.

Native creation stories were protean, and the tease and weave of ironic gestures were badly translated by pioneers, missionaries, federal agents, and scholars. The conceits of these presiding renditions of creation and race linger in familiar conversations as the betrayal of native imagination and liberty. More than two centuries of sorry betrayal have converted some native stories into the uneasy sentiments of victimry. Yet the nostalgia of kitschy victimry can easily be rescripted with more ironic native stories of resistance and survivance.

Native earthdiver stories were totemic, a creative union of storiers, revelers, and later readers, and rightly the stories of risky escapades were never the same. The trickster created a new earth with teases and stories, and the creation was irony, not liturgy. The essence of an oral creation story was not absolute but deferred, and with respect to the tease and creative vision of another native storier. The ethnographic masters forever revise the methods and models of cultural interpretations, and the outcome of research is reported and compared in abstracts, but there are no federal, academic, or monotheistic contracts to bear or break in the creative stories of native ethos, resistance, and survivance over common gossip theory and victimry.

Avishai Margalit declares in *On Betrayal* that a "thick relation" is an element of betrayal. "For betrayal, the harm and the offence must take place between people who are presumed to stand in thick relations," and "thick relations, whether national or personal, are based on a shared past, that it to say, on shared memory."[2] Federal agents and interpreters of native stories were more rangy than thick, and the gossip theories of totemic and cultural relations were undermined by reservation policies of separatism. Surely moral courage and perceptions of irony are better stands for interpretation.

Clarke Chambers, late professor of history at the University of Minnesota, kindly invited me as a new faculty member in American Indian Studies to dinner at his home. He escorted me to a side room and handed over a pair of stained leather moccasins. The historian was serious and expected me to convey the name of the culture and provide some footsy provenance of a surly warrior. "The warrior walked silently in the forests" was my first ironic tease, but the historian was focused more directly on the ethnographic features of the sacred footwear than the tease of an ironic provenance.

I closely examined the beaded decorations, blue beads, first acquired in the ancient fur trade with the French. Deer hide, and the soles were soft and thin, more worn around the house than on game runs in the forest. I then sniffed each moccasin and handed them back to the historian. My voice was resonant, of course, suitable for a discourse on the irony of the outworn moccasins: "Norwegian man, stinky feet, and he walked with a twisted foot."

"Dissembler" and "simulated ignorance" are the original sources of the meaning of irony, according to the *Oxford English Dictionary*. More precisely, irony is defined as the "expression of meaning using language that normally expresses the opposite," especially "the humorous or sarcastic use of praise to imply condemnation or contempt." Figuratively, irony is the discrepancy "between the expected and actual state of affairs" and the "use of language with one meaning for a privileged audience and another for those addressed or concerned" and those excluded in certain cultural situations.[3]

The potentiality of native irony could be observed more critically as a condition embedded in the notes of discovery, in the documents and narratives of dominion, historical archives, ethnographic monographs, the fickle politics of blood quantum, and in the scenes that were once told and translated as traditional stories. These specific sources of irony are actually inside, at the very heart of the narratives, at the core of monographs and archives of native discovery, and not a coy imposition or outsource of irony.

Native stories, creation and otherwise, were seldom delivered as a catechism or liturgy. The many translations and transcriptions of native songs and stories established an archive of disparate narratives, and so many ethnographic interpretations undermined the creative irony and cultural traces of oral stories.

The ethnographic interpretations, however, now provide an unintended source of native irony. Clearly the irony is embedded, and only rarely implied, in the actual methods of transcription, in the general notions of structural analyses, thick or thin descriptions, and in the heavy sway of academic advisors and editors of monographs.

The moccasin game song about "bad moccasins," for instance, was translated and misinterpreted as the lament of a poor native, and with unintended irony. The gestures in the moccasin game songs were about the chance of losing the game, unlucky, not about poverty. The translation of the song must now be delivered as an irony.

The translated song or love charm by a native woman who said she was as beautiful as the roses was actually an ironic song created by a native woman who understood she was not beautiful. Frances Densmore noted in *Chippewa Music* that the singer was "a woman about sixty years of age and was the most dirty and unattractive woman with whom the writer has come in contact." The woman, in a thin and nasal voice, sang in translation, "What are you saying to me? I am arrayed like the roses, and beautiful as they."[4] I favor a more concise and poetic translation, "I am as beautiful as the roses." The pictomyth or song picture shows a heart in a figure surrounded by four roses. Other singers who lived on nearby reservations recognized the pictomyth and sang the same song.

The ancillary sources of native irony, then, are implied in the translations and ethnographic interpretations of oral stories, songs, and narratives by and about natives. The unintended ironies are not derived from outside the native stories or transcriptions but are actually embedded in the medley of ethnographic methods, models, and simulations of natives and in the archives of historical documents.

"Irony and satire provide much keener insights into a group's collective psyche and values that do years of research," observed Vine Deloria Jr. in *Custer Died for Your Sins*. He focused on the humor in stories and the steady cultural tease in native communities. Custer and Columbus were the most common ironic stories in the past fifty years, and natives continue to "come together by sharing humor of the past."[5]

Roger Jourdain, late elected leader of the Red Lake Reservation in Minnesota, met a group of professional women from Minneapolis on tour of the remote reservation. Jourdain welcomed the visitors as they exited the bus. One woman paused and said in a very serious tone of voice, "I have been waiting a long time for an answer to my question: What do Indian women do when they can't nurse their children?" The query revealed the cultural simulations of racial separatism, and the irony was unintended. Jourdain was prepared to provide a comeback that was concise and wry. He kindly told the woman, "Those children were nursed by porcupines."

Ted Mahto, a native philosopher, invited me to trade stories many years ago at Hello Dolly's in Minneapolis. The notorious native bar was sour and sticky that late summer afternoon. At the end of the bar, three young natives were boasting about their scars from a Sun Dance Ceremony. The boasting was contemptible, and my friend excused himself, calmly walked over to the three young men, smiled, slowly unbuttoned his shirt, and pointed to the scars on his chest. Ted said, "Do you see those scars?" The young men leaned closer and examined the prominent scars. Ted shouted, "Chicken pox, 1940," and then turned away, buttoned his shirt, and we continued our stories.

The American Indian Movement carried weapons for the first time in preparation for an armed confrontation with licensed anglers on the opening day of fishing more than forty years ago on the Leech Lake Reservation in Minnesota. The urban militants were heavily armed and determined to fight for native hunting and fishing rights on the reservation, but not prepared for native teases and irony. The militants were not aware that the treaty rights had been decided in favor of the reservation by a federal court.

Dennis Banks, who wore a fur trade mountain man costume, and a dozen other armed leaders were invited to a meeting in an elementary school on the first day they arrived on the reservation. The militants meandered into the classroom and reluctantly sat on tiny chairs, their knees tucked under their chins.

Simon Howard, president of the Minnesota Chippewa Tribe, was the last person to enter the classroom. He sat on a tiny chair at the head of the circle and twirled his thumbs over a heavy stomach. Howard was at home, at ease in a bowling jacket, and he wore a floral print porkpie hat cocked back on his head. The militants were decorated with pantribal war vestments and carried new rifles and other weapons of menace and war. Howard had called the meeting to maintain peace between the local residents, fishermen, and the militants. The strategy to invite the fierce urban warriors to sit on tiny elementary school chairs was shrewd and marvelous.

"Stand up and introduce yourself," said Howard. One shy warrior stood in front of a tiny chair. He was dressed in a wide black hat, leather jacket, dark green glasses, and two bandoliers of heavy ammunition that did not match the bore of his rifle and carried a bayonet and revolver. "We came here to die," he shouted, then returned to the tiny chair.[6]

The sound of heavy rifle fire broke the silence one night on a country road near the Episcopal Church camp. The novel warriors had been invited to stay in the church cabins on treaty land for the duration of the war against white fishermen. Federal marshals conducted a speedy investigation of the rifle fire and revealed that several militants had decided to shine for deer late that night. Seeing what they thought were the bright eyes of a huge deer, the warrior hunters from cities opened fire with advanced weapons. The animal in the dark was a milk cow owned by a local farmer. The farmer fired back at the warriors. Luckily there were no casualties, not even the cow. The warriors were rather new at riflery. The armed warriors seated on tiny chairs were strategic parodies, and the late night cow shoot was an inadvertent irony.

Clyde Kluckholn, cultural anthropologist, was teased as the man who pissed too much on the reservation. Some hitch-hikers on the Navajo Nation told stories about the notorious scholar and his ostensibly weak urinary bladder. Kluckholn asked native hitchhikers about witchcraft and probably reasoned that natives would more readily reveal scenes and secrets of witches and skinwalkers in motion on the road. He listened to witchery rumors and hearsay but could only recollect about thirty minutes of stories. So he frequently stopped and pretended to piss but actually ducked behind a shrub or tree to quickly transcribe in a notebook what he had heard about witches. The natives were no doubt eager to remain in motion, especially at night and in bad weather, and they must have told the gossip theorist whatever stories of witchery that came to mind on the road.[7]

Kluckholn published *Navaho Witchcraft* more than seventy years ago, and the stories of his witchcraft queries and unintended irony continue with great pleasure. One scholarly reviewer pointed out that the anthropologist had described his methods with care, but he did not provide specific information about the "informants." Surely most of his informants were hitchhikers because natives in ordinary situations would rarely mention scary skinwalkers or the ghastly practices of witchery. Other reviewers commended his "method of presentation." The monograph on witchcraft was a betrayal of natives, primarily a collection of simulations derived from hearsay and revised as gossip theory.

Franz Boas, cultural anthropologist, should have been honored by native scholars more than a century ago for his liberal and humanistic observations and teased at the same time for his fraternity as a clever linguistic relativist with no totemic associations and as an extraordinary émigré from Westphalia in Prussia. Franz Boas asserted, "we must fight ceaselessly against the racism that trammels the mind of man" at a faculty luncheon to honor the presence of Paul Rivet, the ethnologist and founder of the Musée de l'Homme in Paris.

Michael Silverstein, distinguished professor of anthropology, linguistics, and psychology at the University of Chicago, related that Boas finished the sentence on racism and then collapsed and died in the Faculty Club at Columbia University on December 21, 1942. His last spoken words about racial and cultural equity were a totemic testament and a scene of linguistic ideology.[8]

Boas wrote in *The Mind of Primitive Man*, "It seems to my mind that the mental attribute of individuals who thus develop the beliefs of a tribe is exactly that of the civilized philosopher," and the "functions of the human mind are common to the whole of humanity." He appreciated the "similar traits in all languages, and also that languages were moulded by thought, not thought by languages."[9] His research and philosophical ideas about language were a critical departure from the ethnocentric notions and gossip theories of the evolution of languages.

Boas pointed out the obvious, "that in many cases a people, without undergoing change in type or mixture, have changed completely their language and culture," as still other "people have retained their language while undergoing material changes in blood and culture." The Athapascan language, for instance, is spoken in several parts of the continent, yet the "forms of culture in these different regions" are distinct. The natives speak the same language but resemble the diverse cultures of California, New Mexico, Arizona, and regions of the Mackenzie River in Canada. "It seems most plausible to assume in this case that branches of this stock migrated from one part of this large area to another, where they intermingled with the neighboring people, and thus changed their physical characteristics, while at the same time they retained their speech."[10]

Michael Silverstein pointed out that "Boas redirects our attention to the 'ethnographical' significance of language and of structural diversity of languages. Language is important not because it is a window on stages of mental and thus cultural evolution. Rather, it is a lens through which we can peer into the fundamental dialectic of human subjectivity, of mind in society—in effect classifying through formal structure what we treat as the 'reality' that surrounds us." Furthermore, "There is always an ontology immanent in a specific linguistic structure."[11]

Silverstein argued that a common dictionary definition of "ideology" is "linguistic ideology in action" and the "codified authority on what words *really* mean," as the nature of authority in the educational establishment, encouraged by publishers. "I should clarify that ideologies about language, or linguistic ideologies, are any sets of beliefs about language articulated by the users as a rationalization or justification of perceived language structure and use" and in general might become "part of divergent large systems of discourse and enterprise."[12]

Edward Sapir and Benjamin Lee Whorf advanced the hypotheses of language and thought. Sapir studied with Franz Boas at Columbia University, and Whorf was a student of Sapir but not an academic linguist. The Sapir-Whorf hypothesis presumes that language and thought structures reality, or "the particular language we speak influences the way we see reality because categories and distinctions encoded in one language are not always available in another language," otherwise understood as linguistic relativity.[13]

Language ideology is not directly related to linguistic relativity, but the general examination of language, culture, and ethos of politics is an obvious connection. Judith Irvine pointed out, "Although the anthropological approach to language ideology is distinctive, it overlaps with research in other disciplines," and since the "concept of language ideology is so fertile, it connects" to many other specialties. She pointed out in her essay on the ideology of language, "there was growing interest in seeing how politics and social action might be embedded in specifics of language structure."[14]

Silverstein asserted, "It is a truism that cultures are essentially social facts, not individual ones; they are properties of populations of people who have come to be, by degrees, tightly or loosely bounded in respect of their groupness, their modes of cohering as a group." Yet is there "a *sociocultural unconscious* in the mind . . . that is both immanent in and emergent from our use of language? Can we ever profoundly study the social significance of language without understanding this sociocultural unconscious that it seem to reveal?"[15] These rhetorical questions of language and the unconscious are related to the sense of natural motion, or native visionary motion, the tease of a totemic presence, and the reveals of unintended irony in narratives construed and concocted with gossip theory.

Ethnographic gossip theories give way to the generous sway of deferred irony in the construal and interpretation of native creation and earthdiver stories and imagistic dream songs. Gossip theories reveal the linguistic ideologies of separatism, dominance, and native victimry.

Jacques Derrida, the French philosopher, introduced the contentious strategy of "deconstruction" to reveal the instability and *différance*, the differed and dissimilarity, or the disparity of meaning in language. Stuart Sim pointed out in *Derrida and the End of History* that deconstruction was a "tactical exercise designed to demonstrate the instability of language and the shaky foundations on which most of our theories rest." Ethnographic gossip theories about natives would surely demonstrate the instability of language and provide the potentiality for narrative irony.

Derrida demonstrated in *différance* the chance and change of meaning, the mutability of language, "which, as he puts it, is always both 'differed' and 'deferred.'" The concept of *différance*, "the manifestation of that instability, is to be found,

Derrida argues, everywhere in our discourse, serving to disrupt our conventional conception of language as a stable medium for the communication of meaning between individuals."[16]

Gossip theory and ethnographic interpretations of natives are not stable conceptions and are surely questionable in the ordinary conferences about natives and others. The methods, models, and simulations of many dissertations endorsed by learned scholars in the academy are not reliable views of native cultures. The deductions are mutable, and the *différance*, or deferred meaning, becomes an ironic disruption of meaning.

Consider, for instance, the gossip theories and erudite narratives that have circumscribed natives for centuries, the thousands of federal agency reports, discovery notes, museum objects, transcribed and translated oral stories, and demographic estimates of early native populations, and grasp that every historical document must be unintended irony because of the chance and mutability of language.

The "object of ethnology," declared Clifford Geertz in *The Interpretation of Cultures*, is a "stratified hierarchy of meaningful structures in terms of which twitches, winks, fake-winks, parodies, rehearsals of parodies are produced, perceived and interpreted." Moreover, culture, "this acted document, thus is public, like a burlesqued wink or a mock sheep raid. Though ideational, it does not exist in someone's head; though unphysical it is not an occult entity."

Geertz declared that the very "concept of culture" is "essentially a semiotic one" and observed that the "ethnographer 'inscribes' social discourse; *he writes it down*. In so doing, he turns it from a passing event, which exists only in its own moment of occurrence, into an account, which exists in its inscriptions and can be reconsulted."[17]

Selected native stories and scenes in contemporary native literature reveal the practices, aspects, and situations of several critical discussions of irony: tragic, fate, situational, naïve, and sarcastic. Native tricksters and other characters or figures in stories, for instance, might pretend to be naïve about the cosmopolitan turns of the world. Poses of silence, overstated traditions, sexuality, and artistic and literary mockery were once common native situations, especially as responses to federal agents and policies, ethnographic studies of native cultural scenes, and now the secretive operations of reservation casinos. Situational irony could be a designer sleeve dog on the reservation, organic wild rice, rubber moccasins, plastic bear claw necklaces, porcupine wet nurses, Pendleton Chief Joseph blankets, Bull Durham ceremonial tobacco, or the Stars and Stripes beaded on a powwow vest. The irony of fate, however, is a complicated situation because chance is a more common sense of native futurity. The native trickster in the familiar earthdiver stories, for instance, creates a new world with bits of sand in the paws and claws of birds and animals.

Tragic irony is situational, actors who played natives in movies, the victimry themes of romance novels, and specific responses of native audiences to movies such as *Cheyenne Autumn*, directed by John Ford in 1964. The Cheyenne were speaking Navajo, a great source of native humor in movie theaters, and others in the audience could not appreciate the tragic or dramatic irony. Consider Jeff Chandler, who played Cochise in *Broken Arrow*, directed by Delmer Daves in 1950. The movie was unintended irony, as a peace treaty was negotiated and a naïve native woman watches with wonder as James Stewart, a very good white man with a magical hand mirror, shaves his face in the great outdoors.

The grasp of irony is crucial to fully recognize the chancy contradictions of historical, political, and critical historical and literary narratives, and the consent of irony creates a lively and humane discourse. The situations of irony in historical narratives are elusive and mostly unintended, and here are two concise instances of unintended dramatic irony. The first case is a historical journey, and the second is literary, the ironic story of a native who never revealed his sacred name, yet his dictated name, a cultural contradiction, is cast in bronze letters on the north façade of Dwinelle Hall at the University of California, Berkeley.

Charles Dickens, novelist and social critic, arrived on the *Messenger*, a sternwheeler steamboat from Pittsburgh to Cincinnati, on April 4, 1842. He mentioned in his journal the great trees and the eternal solitude but not the irony of so many curious names of cities on the Ohio River: Vienna, West Virginia, and Powhatan Point, Syracuse, Portsmouth, Rome, Aberdeen, and Moscow, Ohio. Dickens boarded the steamboat *Zebulon Pike*, which carried the U.S. mail, on April 6, bound for Louisville, Kentucky, and "was a packet of much better class."

Peter Pitchlynn, a native on board that same steamboat, sent his name card to the novelist. The Choctaw leader had been in Washington to secure treaty annuities and was on his way home to a farm near the Wheelock Mission north of the Red River in Indian Territory. Pitchlynn "spoke English perfectly well, though he had not begun to learn the language, he told me, until he was a young man grown," wrote Dickens in *American Notes*. "He was dressed in our ordinary every-day costume, which hung about his fine figure loosely, and with indifferent grace. On my telling him that I regretted not to see him in his own attire, he threw up his right arm, for a moment, as though he were brandishing some heavy weapon, and answered, as he let it fall again, that his race were losing many things besides their dress, and would soon be seen upon the earth no more: but he wore it at home, he added proudly."[18]

Peter Pitchlynn was born on a farm in Mississippi. His father was a prestigious white trader, a frontier diplomat, cotton farmer, and prominent slave owner. Peter was an active politician who became the secretary of the native delegation that negotiated the contentious removal treaty with the federal government at Dancing Rabbit Creek.

Dickens observed that Pitchlynn was "a remarkably handsome man . . . with long black hair, broad cheek-bones, a sunburnt complexion, and a very bright, keen, dark, and piercing eye. There were but twenty thousand of the Choctaws left, he said, and their number was decreasing every day. A few of his brother chiefs had been obliged to become civilized, and to make themselves acquainted with what the whites knew, for it was their only chance of existence."[19]

Dickens wrote about slavery in the last chapter of *American Notes*. "Slavery is not a whit the more endurable because some hearts are to be found which can partially resist its hardening influences; nor can the indignant tide of honest wrath stand still, because in its onward course it overwhelms a few who are comparatively innocent, among a host of guilty."[20] Surely the novelist was not aware at the time that the native he so admired on that steamboat was, in fact, a slave owner and trader.

Dickens wrote in *American Notes* that the Choctaw "took his leave; as stately and complete a gentleman of Nature's making, as ever I beheld; and moved among the people in the boat, another kind of being." Pitchlynn sent the novelist a "lithographed portrait of himself." George Catlin created the portrait print of Peter Pitchlynn.[21]

Ishi was not his sacred native name but a combined first and last nickname. Ishi was named by chance, not by vision, a lonesome native hunter secured almost a century ago by a cultural anthropologist. "He was the last of his tribe," wrote Mary Ashe Miller in the *San Francisco Call* on September 6, 1911. "Probably no more interesting individual could be found today than this nameless Indian."[22]

Alfred Kroeber read the newspaper reports and contacted the sheriff who "had put the Indian in jail not knowing what else to do with him since no one around town could understand his speech or he theirs," wrote Theodora Kroeber. "Within a few days the Department of Indian Affairs authorized the sheriff to release the wild man to the custody of Alfred Kroeber."[23]

Ishi, rescued and named by an anthropologist, lived in rooms furnished by Phoebe Apperson Hearst and worked for five years in the Museum of Anthropology at the University of California in San Francisco. Ishi had endured the unspeakable hate crimes of miners, racial terrorists, and state enabled bounty hunters. Ishi was alone; his family and friends had been murdered. Truly, the miners were the savages, a gruesome irony. California natives barely survived the gold rush, disease, and bounty hunters. Only about fifty thousand natives, or one in five, were alive in the state at the turn of the twentieth century. Alfred Kroeber pointed out that Ishi "has perceptive powers far keener than those of highly educated white men. He reasons well, grasps an idea quickly, has a keen sense of humor, is gentle, thoughtful, and courteous and has a higher type of mentality than most Indians."[24]

Saxton Pope, the surgeon at the medical school located near the museum, wrote that Ishi "amused the interns and nurses by singing" native songs. "His affability and pleasant disposition made him a universal favorite." Ishi "came to the women's wards quite regularly, and with his hands folded before him, he would go from bed to bed like a visiting physician, looking at each patient with quiet concern or with a fleeting smile that was very kindly received and understood."[25] Thomas Waterman, the linguist at the museum, administered various psychological tests and later noted, "this wild man has a better head on him than a good many college men."[26]

The Bureau of Indian Affairs sent a special agent to advise Ishi that he could return to the mountains or live on a government reservation. Kroeber noted that Ishi "shook his head" and said through the interpreter that he would "live like the white people from now on. I want to stay where I am. I will grow old here, and die in this house." And by that he meant his home in the Museum of Anthropology.

Ishi died of tuberculosis five years later, on March 25, 1916. His brain was removed during an autopsy, and the rest of his cremated remains were stored in an urn at the Mount Olivet

Cemetery in Colma, California. Theodora Kroeber reported in *Ishi in Two Worlds* that his estate was divided between the state and the hospital. The dean of the medical school "received two hundred and sixty half dollars."[27]

Ishi Court in Dwinelle Hall was dedicated on May 7, 1993. Gary Strankman, justice of the California First District Court of Appeals, pointed out the obvious irony of memorial names, that for "every student or visitor who can give you some personal history of Wheeler, Boalt, Sproul, or Dwinelle, I can find a hundred, no a thousand, who can tell you the story of Ishi. Without a name he has achieved a fame and a respect that they can only envy."[28]

Mockery is intentional, but situational irony is both intended and unintended, and the condition would be present in every narrative. Consider the millions of books shelved in libraries. The books, some about natives, await readers with new experiences, a sense of responsibility, and the critical capacity to deconstruct the deferred language of narratives, then appreciate the irony. The style, artistic and descriptive language, and the meaning of the words have changed, but the books remain the same, as a memorial of unintended narrative irony. The irony is unintended, of course, because most authors could not have anticipated the deferred meaning and *différance* of language.

The dominance of discovery, sway of social science narratives, power of archives, and authority of government documents created a simulated sense of the familiar, a final ethnographic vocabulary about natives, and the necessary deconstruction of the familiar was the course of irony.

Jonathan Lear in *A Case for Irony* named this uncanny experience of unfamiliarity an "ironic disruption" because what was once "taken as familiar" has "suddenly become unfamiliar" and pointed out that his "*practical knowledge*" was disrupted in an "ironic moment." Lear observed that there was "something about my practical identity that breaks my practical identity apart: it seems larger than, disruptive of, itself." He distinguished *the experience of irony* from a *capacity for irony*" as a "peculiar experience" that is personal, but not in the sense that all experience is first person. The experience of *"practical knowledge* is disrupted" in an "ironic moment."[29] Lear declared that the capacity for irony is clearly to experience irony, but he does not consider the contrasts of intended and unintended irony or the chance and peculiar experience of an ironic disruption in ethnographic studies of natives.

Victor Barnouw recorded hundreds of trickster stories and published them in *Wisconsin Chippewa Myths and Tales*. From "these stories," he observed, "we can learn something about the belief systems of the people who told and listened to them." Barnouw declared that the trickster "was a real person whom they respected although they also laughed at his antics." Trickster stories are visionary and about a wild, lusty, fantastic figure who creates a new world. The trickster as "a real person" is reductive, mere gossip theory, and an ethnographic betrayal of native stories, but the concoction is a source of unintended irony.

Tom Badger, an ethnographic fictional name, told trickster creation stories that were recorded at Lac du Flambeau in Wisconsin and published some seventy years ago. Julia Badger, his wife, was the interpreter. Badger told Barnouw about the trickster Wenebojo, or Naanabozho, who was standing on the top of a tree, in a creation story: "He had his head back, and the water was up to his mouth. Pretty soon Wenebojo felt that he wanted to defecate. He couldn't hold it. The shit floated up to the top of the water and floated around his mouth. After a while Wenebojo noticed that there was an animal in the water. This animal was playing around. Wenebojo couldn't see the animal, but he knew that it was there. He tried to look around. Then he saw several animals—beaver, muskrat, and otter. Wenebojo spoke to the otter first, 'Brother,' he said, 'could you go down and get some earth? If you do that, I will make an earth for you and me to live on.'"

Barnouw evaluated the ironic earthdiver trickster stories of creation with psychoanalytic gossip theories that ruined the moment of the stories, but the interpretation and publication of the stories contributed to an incredible source of unintended irony, a source of much humor in a more secure native academic world seventy years later.

Barnouw observed that "Tom Badger was a reserved, intelligent, mild-mannered man in his seventies. . . . I gave him a Rorschach Test and collected two Draw-a-Person drawings. . . . The man's head was drawn very large in relation to the rest of the body, and there was a strong emphasis on the mouth, while the arms were weakly depicted. Moreover, although Tom said that the man was naked, he was given no sexual organs." Barnouw was an ethnographer, and he carried out his academic duties with no obvious sense of irony, deferred, differed, or not, and he could not have been aware of gossip theory or linguistic ideology.

Werner Wolff, a psychologist, "suggested that Tom Badger was probably a passive, dreamy person, with sexual inhibitions and that perhaps the frustration in the sexual sphere resulted in a transfer to the oral region." Pauline Vorhaus analyzed the Rorschach record and "remarked that there was evidence of emotional dependency and also some confusion about sex, since Tom's form level was good except for the sexual responses. The two interpretations suggest the existence of repression, which is also suggested by the origin myth, with its avoidance of women and sex and its recurrent oral and anal themes."[30]

Barnouw and others carried out at least four unreliable applications of scrutiny and gossip theory that countered the native visionary character of earthdiver stories and storiers: Tom Badger is a disguise, a fictional name; the real storier might have been a dubious storier, solitary, or disconnected; his wife might have been a tedious or unreliable translator; and the eager academic ethnographer favored the gossip theory of anal folklore over visionary trickster stories, an obvious linguistic ideology.

Dennis Tedlock, literary scholar and anthropologist, considered native stories as art, not a clinical or comparative subject, and wrote that storiers were "not merely repeating memorized words" or presenting a "concert reading" but rather an art performance, and "we are getting the *criticism* at the same time and from the same person. The interpreter does not merely play the parts, but is the narrator and commentator as well."[31]

Barnouw pointed out that there "seems to be more emphasis on the anal zone in the folklore," and "Freudians find an explanation for the 'anal character' in severe early toilet training, but one would not expect to find strict toilet training in a 'nomadic' tribal culture." Perhaps "we should not see the presence of anal motifs as something surprising or pathological. After all, an interest in feces is natural and understandable."[32]

Barnouw noted that Alan Dundas, folklorist at the University of California, Berkeley, "suggested that the earthdiver motif is a male fantasy of creation stemming from male envy of female pregnancy and an assumed cloacal theory." Moreover, this "may seem an extravagant hypothesis, but it would be in keeping with the Chippewa myth with its exclusion of women and its striking anal themes."[33]

"Despite the lack of a great number of actual excremental myths," observed Dundas, "the existence of any at all would appear to lend support to the hypothesis that men do think of creativity in anal terms, and further that this conception is projected into mythical cosmogenic terms." The concept of coprophilia, the abnormal pleasure of feces, was based on the "existence of a cloacal theory of birth, and the existence of pregnancy envy on the part of males."[34]

The trickster stories of an earthdiver creation have clearly captured the cloacal interests of several serious academics. The earthdiver stories were creative and ironic, and in translation these stories continue to be delightful literary parodies, but not the concoctions of psychodrama or psychographic revisionism. The gossip theory of *merde* manners and cloacal speculation has become a great source of unintended irony.

The winter creation stories might have been weather diversions. The scenes were more urgent on a cold night with the insistence of a bowel movement in an outhouse or at the very moment a new island world was about to be constructed with a forepaw of sand and mire. The cloacal psychobabble has become a collection of academic earthdiver stories with the untold excreta of unintended irony.

The monographs of ethnographic gossip theories and betrayal of natives have ultimately provided an enormous source of unintended irony and the promise of mockery. Thousands of academic dissertations and conference papers on native cultures and stories await the deconstruction and ironic disruptions of linguistic ideologies and final academic vocabularies.

Victor Barnouw and Alan Dundas, if they were alive today, would surely commence a cloacal critique of the current exhibition of weighty fecal specimens and mucky stories at the National Poo Museum, the first comparative and formal *merde* exhibition in the world. United Press International reported, "The museum, which officially opened to the public on the Isle of Wight, was created by the Eccleston George artist collective using animal and human droppings donated by members of the public and the Isle of Wight Zoo and Dinosaur Isle Museum."[35] This new tease of fecal creation stories is a marvelous ironic disruption of the cloacal gossip theories in the world.

[2]

Survivance and Liberty

Turns and Stays of Native Sovereignty

The Great Peace of Montréal has become a mainstay in the early historical and literary references to the continental liberty and cultural sovereignty of natives in colonial North America. Native American peace and liberty were at the heart of the best stories of creation, and clearly in trickster stories of the woodland Anishinaabe, Ojibwe, Ojibwas, or Chippewa, but these sentiments of autonomy were seldom mentioned in the federal treaties of power, removal, racial and cultural separation, and the exploitation of natural resources on treaty reservations.

The early histories of northern natives were fraught with the complicity of the fur trade, the deceit of colonial politics, and wars of continental dominion, and at the same time, natives endured several waves of lethal diseases that decimated families and communities and weakened the very practices of traditional native healers. A century later natives endured racial separatism in a constitutional democracy, yet the earlier ratification of a singular peace treaty provided a respite from the commune crusades for two or three native generations. That singular treaty of ethos, moral imagination, and peace was the start of new native stories of survivance and liberty.

Louis-Hector de Callière, the governor general of New France, convened Ouabangué, a representative of Ojibwas or Saulteurs, Chichicatalo, a representative of the Miamis, and more than thirty other native ambassadors, cultural envoys, visionaries, warriors, orators, and peacemakers to endorse the treaty of peace with formal signatures and totemic marks on August 4, 1701.

More than a thousand natives traveled for days and weeks by canoe to attend an extraordinary peace convention on the Saint Lawrence River near Montréal. The native "representatives of forty distinct nations put their signatures to *La Grande Paix de Montréal*," observed Gilles Harvard in *The Great Peace of Montreal of 1701*. France was the only colonial nation at the peace conference, and the other nations were native "from the vast area extending from Acadia to the eastern edge of the Great Lakes."[1]

The great treaty of peace continued for almost sixty years, or until the French were defeated on the Plains of Abraham and the British seized Montréal on September 8, 1760. The moral imagination of that peace convention, the first native entente cordiale, clearly demonstrated the civility and respect of native liberty, and that honorable principle has continued as a mainstay in early native stories, histories, and literature.

The French recognized the independence but not the absolute sovereignty of natives because native nations were not dominions or states; however, the French negotiated with natives "in the same way that they negotiated in Europe, by signing proper treaties," noted Harvard.[2] Governor Callière initiated the peace treaty and sent emissaries to invite native leaders as far away as the Great Lakes to attend the conference in Montréal. The native "ambassadors were never picked at random. Among the Iroquois," noted Harvard, "they were the best orators and not always the hereditary chiefs. The same was apparently true among the Amerindians of the Great Lakes."[3]

Harvard declared that the Great Peace of Montréal should

not be read only as an analysis of the agreements because the document of peace "provides a striking and evocative image of French colonization in North America. The gathering of thirteen hundred Amerindians from as far away as the Mississippi Valley and Acadia . . . is a reflection of the relative success of the French colonial enterprise at the dawn of the eighteenth century. In spite of their small population, the French had managed to extend their influence over a large part of the continent."[4]

Native property rights and the pushy queries of who owned the land in North America were more difficult concepts than the theories of sovereignty or the power and duties of governance. That critical contrast "between the two concepts was not drawn as sharply in the seventeenth century as it is today," wrote Stuart Banner in *How the Indians Lost Their Land*, "but the notion that the heathens lacked property rights was controversial, even in the earliest years of colonization."[5]

The Great Peace of Montréal respected the liberty and distinctive cultures of natives and concentrated more on the peace of trade routes and commerce than on the concepts of property and sovereignty. New France explorers, traders, and diplomats respected the territorial rights and interest of natives. Banner observed, "The danger posed by the French, if the English insufficiently respected Indian property rights, came to the fore in the middle of the eighteenth century, when the illegal encroachments of English settlers on Indian land drove many tribes to ally with France."[6]

David E. Wilkins noted in *The White Earth Nation* that there were many nominations and adaptations of native sovereignty in judicial narratives, federal reports and policy, and literature. He considered variations of "indigenous sovereignty," including savage, quasi, spiritual, cultural, ancient, artistic, and many other concepts and revisions of native sovereignty: "Such a plethora of terms makes it difficult to gain any clear and sensible understanding of the actual status of indigenous nations; their inherent authority in internal and external powers."[7]

The French fur traders built small posts in a vast area between Lake Winnipeg and Lake of the Woods to the Great Lakes and Montréal and emerged as a unique configuration of an empire in North America. "The French did not really occupy the area they now claimed; in fact, much of it they did not yet claim," observed W. J. Eccles in *The Canadian Frontier*. The French voyaged in the seventeenth century through the rivers and lakes of North America and traded with "Indians, obtain a cargo of furs, then transport it back to Montreal. The Indians were the important factor. It was they who provided the desired commodity." Consequently, "their interests, their traditional way of life, their seminomadic hunting economy, had to be preserved. Yet the Indian's way of life was radically altered. Tribes ever more remote became enmeshed in the European economic empire and became dependent on European goods. They achieved a somewhat higher standard of living, but ultimately paid a very heavy price for it."[8]

The United States negotiated treaties in contested areas of settlement but seldom with respect for native property rights, liberty, or cultures. Stuart Banner observed that it was "increasingly apparent by the middle of the nineteenth century that many of the treaties in which tribes ostensibly consented to live on reservations were not treaties in the full sense of the word, but documents papering over the exercise of force."

William Dole, commissioner of Indian affairs, for instance, argued in "his annual report for 1862, 'It may well be questioned whether the government has not adopted a mistaken policy in regarding the Indian tribes as quasi-independent nations, and making treaties with them for the purchase of the lands they claim to own.' Dole suggested, 'They have none of the elements of nationality; they are within the limits of the recognized authority of the United States and must be subject to its control.'"[9]

Native treaties were constantly exposed to political debate and criticism, and the concept of native sovereignty was never clearly decided in the courts or by congressional resolutions. Banner noted that despite the criticism, "the federal government had continued to enter into treaties with Indian tribes. There were always white humanitarian voices to speak up for treaties, because any other method of acquiring the Indians' land promised to leave the Indians even worse off. But the growing realization in the mid-nineteenth century that many of the new treaties were shams had the effect of muting this kind of support."[10]

The White Earth Reservation was established by treaty on March 19, 1867. The Minnesota treaty was not about peace but rather a declaration that removed natives from other familiar family settlements. Ten native leaders and several federal agents ratified the treaty, and natives with diverse dialects and totemic associations were removed from several sections of the state and consigned to the new White Earth Reservation.

The eight articles of the removal treaty provided for federal services, a physician, schools and houses, horses, farm equipment, sawmill, annuities, and certified allotments of land on 1,300 square miles, or more than three thousand square kilometers, of land in northern Minnesota. Currently natives own less than 15 percent of that treaty reservation land, yet the treaty boundaries remained the same in federal court decisions.

The treaty provisions clearly represented the policies of cultural assimilation, not the moral imagination of a peace treaty. Many native families removed to the White Earth Reservation were descendants of fur traders, literate in two languages and probably one regional trade language, and forever documented in history with the distinctive surnames of New France.

Peace was not the primary mission of the treaty nor the cause of other federal treaties with natives. More than three hundred executive treaties were constructed with natives from the Treaty with the Delaware in 1778 to the Fort Laramie Treaty in 1868. Some were removal treaties and others circumscribed pueblos and other indigenous regions.

The crude ideology of separatism, dominance, and federal treaty politics were generally comparable to the theory of cognitive dissonance, or the inconsistent colonial course of racial and cultural separatism and, at the same time, the homespun enactment of national assimilation policies. Natives were coerced to become yeoman farmers on treaty reservations under the absolute authority of federal agents.

The dissonance of federal policies was never absolved in the discussions of moral imagination, native peace, and liberty and seldom mentioned in the ordinary settlement hearsay or even the gossip theories of experts on natives and colonial policy. The analogies of cognitive dissonance have continued and yet federal agents hardly noticed the favor of ironic native stories of liberty on treaty reservations. The secretary of Indian affairs, for instance, has continued the dissonance and declined to publically support the new Constitution of the White Earth Nation.

The treaties of removal and dominance were federal practices of political trickery and not comparable to the negotiated treaties of peace. The Great Peace of Montréal was ratified with the moral imagination of native orators, ambassadors, and emissaries, and the treaty represented the moral duties and responsibilities of traders and native nations. The crude executive treaties of removal and separatism were never inspired by moral imagination or the ethos of governance. The autocratic maneuvers of federal agents represented only the deceit of liberalism, abuse of pluralism, and cruel ironies of a democratic constitution.

"The project of advancing tribal sovereignty in the United States through a revitalized ethos of legal pluralism encounters another, perhaps deeper, set of questions about the compatibility of pluralism and liberalism," argued the legal scholar N. Bruce Duthu in *Shadow Nations: Tribal Sovereignty and the Limits of Legal Pluralism*. He discussed the challenges of the concepts of liberalism, liberty, individuality, and equality in the "broader category" of native sovereignty and the rights of governance. "The challenge for liberals," he observed, "has been to locate a principled basis for supporting indigenous rights within the predominate political ideology of our time."[11]

David Bromwich discussed moral imagination as a human faculty and individual spirit rather than as a cultural practice, and the "power that compels us to grant the highest possible reality and the largest conceivable claim to a thought, action, or person that is not our own, and not close to us in any obvious way. The force of the idea of moral imagination is to deny that we can ever know ourselves sufficiently to settle on a named identity that prescribes our conduct or affiliations. Moral imagination therefore seems to me inseparable from the freedom that is possible in society."[12] That sense of moral imagination is similar to the sentiments of native stories of survivance and continental liberty provided in the Great Peace of Montréal.

The Articles of Confederation and the Constitution of the United States were created by the absolute integrity of a revolution. The Constitution of Japan, a ratified document of comparable democratic governance, was created by an extraordinary military order. General Douglas MacArthur, the supreme commander of the Allied Powers that occupied Japan at the end of the Second World War, directed his senior officers to create a constitution that renounced war, abolished feudalism, and provided suffrage for women and protection of diverse political parties. That masterly document was drafted with moral imagination in about two weeks' time and became the lasting democratic Constitution of Japan.

The Constitution of the White Earth Nation was written by a principal native writer and with the inspiration of forty sworn delegates who were moved with moral imagination to create the necessary articles of an egalitarian government. The constitution was not created by revolution or ordered by the supreme command of an occupation general or by a federal agency.

Erma Vizenor, elected chief of the White Earth Reservation government, was determined to transform the corporate and executive style of governance imposed by the federal government in favor of a new egalitarian constitution with a balance of executive and legislative powers and a judiciary directed by principles of native reciprocity rather than retribution. The Constitution of the White Earth Nation was duly ratified by the official delegates and then certified by almost 80 percent of the native citizens who voted in a referendum.

The "massive surge in constitutional writing (and in some cases rewriting) produced the greatest number of constitutions ever devised in an equivalent length of time in the history of the world," declared Wilkins, the native constitutional scholar. He observed that the "White Earth Nation, long a part of the confederated arrangement with the other Anishinaabeg polities, has arrived at the realization that they have matured to the point of devising a document to encompass their present-day understanding of political, legal, economic, and cultural autonomy."[13]

Constitutional democracies have not always been the source of moral imagination or liberty. The easy promises of egalitarian governance are political and deceptive, and even when natives by their own moral imagination create a constitution, the document does not absolve the cognitive dissonance of political corruption, dubious blood rights, or federal policies.

"Democracy stirs in the wake of American armies," declared Jacques Rancière in *Hatred of Democracy*. This bold assertion and the ironic democratic responses to military dominance were more noticeable in native stories of the past than in the current critical comments about American armies and corporations in the Middle East and Central Asia. The "arguments used to back up the military campaigns devoted to the worldwide rise of democracy reveal the paradox concealed by the dominant usage of the word today," noted Rancière. Democracy "would appear to have two adversaries. On the one hand, it is opposed to a clearly identified enemy—arbitrary government, government without limits—which, depending on the moment, is referred to either as tyranny, dictatorship, or totalitarianism. But this self-evident opposition conceals another, more intimate, one. A good democratic government is one capable of controlling the evil quite simply called democratic life."[14]

The Anishinaabe and many other native cultures have endured the empires and convey the memories, stories, and historical ironies of three world wars. The first was in the late eighteenth century in North America. The second was in France, and the third was in Europe and Japan.

More than twenty thousand natives served in the American Civil War a century after the termination of the Great Peace of Montréal. Most natives served the Union, but the Creek, Choctaw, and other native nations owned slaves and served with the Confederacy. General Ely S. Parker, Seneca diplomat and attorney, created the concise articles of surrender that General Robert E. Lee signed on April 9, 1865, at Appomattox Court House. Parker had served as military secretary to General Ulysses S. Grant and was promoted to brevet brigadier general. Grant was elected president four years later and appointed Parker the commissioner of Indian affairs.

Natives enlisted and were drafted, more than fifteen thousand of them, and served with distinction in the First World War. After serious political debates about racial separation in the military, natives were not segregated in the American Expeditionary Forces. More than twenty-five thousand native soldiers served in the Second World War.

Private William Hole in the Day, for instance, was born on the White Earth Reservation. He was a direct relative of the great spiritual leader Bugonaygeshig, or Hole in the Day. William was determined about the military and first served in the United States Navy during the Spanish-American War and later served in the North Dakota National Guard on the Mexican border. Hole in the Day enlisted in Canada and served in the First Central Ontario Regiment in the Canadian Expeditionary Forces in France. He could not wait for the United States to declare war against the Empire of Germany. Hole in the Day was poisoned in a gas attack at the Battle of Passchendaele early in the war and died on June 4, 1919, at the Canadian General Hospital in Montréal.

Private Ignatius Vizenor was born on May 14, 1894, on the White Earth Reservation. He entered military service on February 25, 1918, and served in the 118th Infantry Regiment attached to the British Expeditionary Forces in France. He was killed in action on October 8, 1918, in Montbréhain, France. Ignatius was buried in Saint Benedict Catholic Cemetery on the White Earth Reservation.[15]

Thomas Britten noted in *American Indians in World War I* that military service "was a catalyst for change. Few of the young men who entered stateside army training camps or stepped onto the battlefields of France returned home without having acquired new insights and attitudes." Many soldiers were wounded, scarred in spirit and body, and forever burdened with gruesome memories of war. Yet "others gained a sense of purpose, discipline, and pride" as soldiers in France, observed Britten. "In some ways, therefore, military service accomplished many of the objectives set by assimilationists."[16]

Thousands of natives returned from military service in both world wars with new experiences and moved to cities around the country. First World War veterans returned to reservation poverty, and many moved to cities, but there were very few jobs for veterans and fewer opportunities for natives. Many natives were more literate than other military veterans because they had attended federal and mission boarding schools, some three generations of natives attended school before national compulsory education.

The Great Depression of the early 1930s caused severe poverty on reservations and drove more natives to large cities. Similarly, many native veterans remained in cities, some attended colleges, and others received occupational training after the Second World War. Minneapolis, for instance, became a crucial refuge for thousands of natives from northern reservations. By the 1960s an estimated five thousand natives, more than twice the population of the White Earth Reservation, lived in what became known as the "urban reservation." Many other cities, Denver, Los Angeles, Phoenix, Chicago, and Oakland, for instance, became the destination of thousands of natives from reservations around the country. The federal treaties were no longer relevant after economic depressions, wars, and extreme poverty.

Winifred Jourdain, one of the most prominent and memorable grandmothers of the Anishinaabe, was born July 31, 1900, on the White Earth Reservation. She encouraged the sentiments of survivance, overcame the politics of poverty, and moved with many other natives to Minneapolis during the Great Depression. Alice Beaulieu Vizenor, my paternal grandmother, also left the reservation with her family at about the same time in search of work in Minneapolis.

The concept of survivance is elusive, imprecise by definition, translation, comparison, and by catchword histories, but the sentiment of the word is invariably true and just in native stories, practice, and company. Survivance is as complex as the notions and course of dominance.

The nature of survivance, however, is unmistakable in native stories, natural reason, remembrance, and traditions and clearly observed in spirited resistance and individual attributes, such as the native tease, vital irony, cast of mind, and moral imagination and courage. Survivance creates an actual sense of native presence over absence, over nihility, and denies the reductive themes of victimry that are all too common in journalism and popular literature.[17]

Charles Aubid, for instance, declared in stories his native presence, human rights, and sovereignty. He created a sense of survivance in federal court, defied the rule of hearsay and judicial precedent, and countered the cultural absence of natives and popular themes of victimry. The inspired storier was a sworn witness in federal court that autumn more than forty years ago in Minneapolis. He raised his hand and listened to the oath for the first time in the language of the Anishinaabe. Then he waved his hand, an ironic gesture of the oath, at the presiding Federal District Court Judge Miles Lord.

Aubid was a witness in a dispute with the federal government over the right to regulate the actual harvest of *manoomin*, or wild rice, on the Rice Lake National Wildlife Refuge in Minnesota. Federal agents had assumed the authority to determine the wild rice season and to regulate the harvest, a bureaucratic action that natives resisted with a sense of cultural survivance, experience, and sovereignty.

Aubid, who was eighty-six years old at the time of his testimony in federal court, related through translators that he was present as a young man when the federal agents told Old John Squirrel that the Anishinaabe would always have control of the *manoomin* harvest. Aubid demonstrated in court that natives conveyed and understood their rights in stories. Old John Squirrel was there in the memories of Aubid, a visionary presence in the stories of native survivance. The court could have heard the testimony as a visual trace of an oral agreement, clearly a function of memorable and judicial discourse, both relevant and in that instance necessary.

Justice Lord, however, agreed at first with the objection of the federal attorney that the testimony was hearsay and not admissible. The judge explained to the witness that the court cannot hear as evidence what a dead man said, only the actual experiences of the witness. "John Squirrel is dead," said the judge. "And you can't say what a dead man said."

Aubid turned brusquely in the witness chair, bothered by what Justice Lord had said about Old John Squirrel. Aubid pointed at the legal books on the bench, then he shouted in English that those books contained the stories of dead white men. "Why should I believe what a white man says, when you don't believe John Squirrel?"

Judge Lord was deferential, amused by the analogy of native stories to court testimony, the concepts of precedent and hearsay, and judicial traditions. "You've got me there," said the judge.[18]

The Anishinaabe have imagined for more than a century a new liberty and a representative government of survivance on the White Earth Reservation. At the same time, native men and women have served with honor in the military before they were recognized as citizens of the United States with the passage of the Indian Citizenship Act of 1924.

The Constitution of the White Earth Nation is a communal and steadfast response to the service of natives and the sustained visions of survivance and liberty. The constitution was duly ratified by sworn delegates and then approved and adopted by a referendum vote of recognized citizens on November 19, 2013.

I was one of forty delegates sworn to serve on the constitutional convention. I declared at the first of four conventions, convened over two years, that schoolchildren one day would study the historic creation of a democratic constitution of the White Earth Nation. I was later named the principal writer of the new constitution.

The Anishinaabe once created dream songs, or oral imagistic poetry, to honor their totemic associations with nature, and one of the most memorable dream songs, "I feel the summer in the spring," has become a suitable reference to the new Constitution of the White Earth Nation. The Anishinaabe perceived and celebrated seasonal changes in visions, dream songs, and creation stories. The appreciation and ethos of these necessary and unequivocal celebrations of natural motion and change, the sentiments of survivance, reciprocity, totemic associations with animal and birds, and native liberty were declared in the ratified articles of the new Constitution of the White Earth Nation.

The White Earth Reservation was established by treaty in 1867. Twenty years later, in 1887, my relatives published the first independent weekly newspaper on the White Earth Reservation. Augustus Hudon Beaulieu, publisher of *The Progress* and later a new newspaper named *The Tomahawk*, vigorously resisted the Dawes General Allotment Act. His two newspapers published editorial articles that opposed the individual allotment of communal native land, and they challenged the concoction of blood quantum to carry out the dubious notions and federal policies of cultural assimilation.

The preamble to the Constitution of the White Earth Nation is presented in two articles. The first article celebrates the traditional sentiments of survivance and cultural sovereignty, and the second declares the provisions to secure the inherent rights of the citizens of the White Earth Nation:

> The Anishinaabeg of the White Earth Nation are the successors of a great tradition of continental liberty, a native constitution of families, totemic associations. The Anishinaabeg create stories of natural reason, of courage, loyalty, humor, spiritual inspiration, survivance, reciprocal altruism, and native cultural sovereignty.
>
> We the Anishinaabeg of the White Earth Nation in order to secure an inherent and essential sovereignty, to promote traditions of liberty, justice, and peace, and reserve common resources, and to ensure the inalienable rights of native governance for our posterity, do constitute, ordain and establish this Constitution of the White Earth Nation.

The Constitution of the White Earth Nation creates a sense of individual and collective sovereignty and is truly a government for the people, and the people determine how to represent their interests through three distinct and separate divisions of the government, the executive, legislative, and judicial. The constitution contains twenty chapters and 118 specific articles on the rights of the citizens and the duties of the elected government.

The forty delegates to the constitutional conventions were mostly elders, more than sixty years of age. More than half of the sworn delegates were residents of reservation communities. No delegates were lawyers. Two delegates were nominated at large. More than half the delegates had completed college courses through extension education on the reservation, and twelve of the forty had earned one or more academic degrees. Two were college teachers, one was a retired fireman, two worked in health services, and another was a musician.

The moral imagination, heartfelt ideas of native liberty, natural motion and change, ethos of governance, and the sentiments of survivance and sovereignty were embraced in the egalitarian articles of the Constitution of the White Earth Nation.

Native Transmotion

Totemic Motion and Traces of Survivance

The concept of transmotion, a spirited and visionary sense of natural motion, has evolved into an aesthetic theory to interpret the modes, distinctions, and traces of motion in sacred objects, stories, art, and literature.[1] The migration of birds, aerial maneuvers of starlings, tease of ravens, dive of water ouzels in a cold mountain stream, shadows in the snow, shimmer of light on a wet spider web, blue shadows in the snow, traces of the seasons, and the tropes of native totemic animals and birds are unmissable scenes of natural motion in native creation stories, visionary dream songs, and literature.

Transmotion is related to the ordinary practices of survivance, a philosophical conviction that is derived from the critical examination of sacred objects in museums and relative observations of motion and totemic associations in art, literature, and languages.

Cultural survivance is an obvious resistance to the pushy ideologies of nationalism, ethnographic simulations and models, and gossip theory. The visionary and totemic stories of creation are instances of literary transmotion, and continuous variations of origin stories create a distinct sense of presence and survivance.

My literary mediations and theories on transmotion and

survivance arise from critical studies of the concocted provenance of sacred objects, actual totemic visions and associations, stories of the fur trade, situational narratives, contemporary native literature, and from perceptions and descriptions of cosmototemic art. Native creation stories, totemic visions, sacred objects, dreams, and nicknames are heard daily and remembered as transcendent traces of cultural survivance.

The actual practices of survivance create a vital and astute sense of presence over absence in history, stories, art, and literature. "The nature of survivance creates a sense of narrative resistance to absence, literary tragedy, nihility, and victimry. Native survivance is an active sense of presence over historical absence" and the manifest manners of monotheism and cultural dominance. Native survivance is a continuance of visionary stories.[2]

The traces of totemic or visionary transmotion are clearly observable in indigenous cavern art, on ancient stone, and in the contemporary portrayals by many native painters and literary artists. The painterly features of transmotion, however, are original and rather elusive. Yet the traces of totemic transmotion are easily perceived in the imagination, interpretation, and translations of songs, stories, and literary art.

The Anishinaabe word *manidooke* means in translation "to have a spiritual power" and "to conduct a ceremony." The word is an "animate intransitive verb" and describes a visionary sense of motion and presence.[3] The wider sense of the word is construed as spiritual and visionary motion, or transmotion and survivance. The natural motion is not constrained or determined by a direct syntactical object.

"The sky loves to hear me sing" is a vital revelation of natural motion in an Anishinaabe dream song.[4] The native singer listens to the turnout of the seasons, then directs the words of his song to the natural motion or the wind and sky. The gesture is ironic, of course, a gratifying tease of nature and a creative totemic sense of presence.

"With a large bird above me, I am walking in the sky" and "I feel the summer in the spring" are translations of two more visionary songs that were heard more than a century ago among the Anishinaabe in northern Minnesota.[5]

Frances Densmore translated these dream songs in *Chippewa Music* at the turn of the twentieth century. She recorded hundreds of native singers on phonographic cylinders, the most advanced recording technology at the time, and provided stories of the songs, translations by the singers, and ethnographic notes. Densmore recorded "Song of the Crows" by Henry Selkirk, for instance. He explained that the song was a gift. Clearly the singer assumes the voice and visionary transmotion of the crow and arrives with the turn of the seasons.

The first to come
I am called
Among the birds
I bring the rain
Crow is my name[6]

Natural motion is easily grasped in the singular tropes and gestures of innovative literature, but the pleasures of ironic motion are hardly perceived in ordinary comparative similes, such as "walks like a duck," "eats like a dog," or "dumb as a donkey." Comparative similes are facile and sideline the tropes of natural motion in songs and stories.

"Overhanging clouds, echoing my words, with a pleasing sound, across the earth, everywhere, making my voice heard" and "the first to come, epithet among the birds, bringing the rain, crow is my name" are ironic dream songs and tropes of natural motion by a nineteenth century native Anishinaabe.[7]

Kobayashi Issa, the generous haiku poet of eighteenth century Japan, created a poignant image about the death of his young daughter: "the world of dew, is the world of dew, and yet . . . and yet."[8] The imagistic scene creates a natural sense of motion, a world of dew, and at the same time the tropes of memory and impermanence. The scene is elusive and in motion, not a descriptive contrast or closure.

Stephen Addiss in *The Art of Haiku* provided a rather reductive interpretation that the image "captures the moment when sincere religious understanding meets the deepest feeling of the heart." The natural motion of that concise image of sorrow and a world of dew was not a captured scene; instead the scene continues as a visionary motion of memory.[9]

Native stories tease a natural and visionary sense of presence, an ironic presence, and create elusive images of natural motion that are clearly more than the simulations of similitude and sincerity, more than the conventions of cultural intrigue, adventures, or petitions of commercial literary victimry. Native stories are not priestly liturgies. The stories of creation and the marvelous scenes of visionary motion or transmotion are related to visual memories, and without recitations, storyline structures, plot resolutions, shibboleths of character development, or the denouement of commercial literature.

Commercial native literature has commonly been structured with the familiar themes of tragedy and victimry, but with scarcely any consideration of classical irony or comedy. Native stories, however, are imagined and related with a sense of natural motion and survivance, and not with the cultural salvation of monotheism or tragic denouement of victimry. The commercial editors of the most saleable themes of romantic victimry have obligated many native writers to convert a sense of survivance to scenes of absence and victimry as a condition of publication, including the renunciation of survivance in the popular *Black Elk Speaks*, transcribed by John Neihardt, and the unsuitable revisions of victimry in *The Surrounded* by D'Arcy McNickle.

Toni Jensen writes with a sense of transmotion and native survivance in "At the Powwow Hotel," a short story published in *From the Hill*: "When the cornfield arrived, I was standing in our hotel's kitchen, starting Lester's birthday cake. It was rain-ing outside, foggy too, for the sixth day in a row, and there was flour all over my blue jeans. . . . We live in West Texas on a three-hundred-acre cotton farm at the edge of Blanco Canyon. We own the Blanco Canyon Hotel, all twelve rooms, though everybody in town calls it the Powwow Hotel on account of Lester and me being Indian."[10] Other natives arrived at the hotel that day, and the conversations continued with gestures to the miraculous arrival of corn, a field of corn. The Navajos "talked about why the corn had skipped them, had set its course east of their tribes."

"But tonight," the narrator declares, "there was the sound of feet, moving counterclockwise, the smell of coffee and bread and the raw, greenness of the field. And tonight, there were my legs, still at first, but surprising me by doing anything at all, and then there I was, part of it, moving." Jensen created a marvelous sense of natural motion and cultural survivance. The arrival of the corn is a crucial and memorable scene of totemic and visionary transmotion at the Powwow Hotel.[11]

Leslie Marmon Silko in her novel *Ceremony* encircles the reader with mythic witches, ironic creation stories, and a sense of natural motion. "That is the trickery of the witchcraft," said the old man. "They want us to believe all evil resides with white people. They will look no further to see what is really happening. They want us to separate ourselves from white people, to be ignorant and helpless as we watch our own destruction. But white people are only tools that the witchery manipulates; and I tell you, we can deal with white people, with their machines and their beliefs. We can because we invented white people; it was Indian witchery that made white people in the first place."[12] The witches contrived a customary binary structure of race, a mythic cultural separation. The literary witchery is ironic, a trace of transmotion in a contemporary creation story.

"I have no state but my visionary portrayals in art, no native nation but a sensual, totemic landscape of memories, and the unreserved resistance to dominance and nostalgia," declared Dogroy Beaulieu, the native artist and narrator of my recent novel *Shrouds of White Earth.* "Does anyone ever experience a native state, a secure place of stories, solace, and sentiments that never torment the heart and memories? Yes, of course, my friend, you create marvelous literary scenes and stories of the reservation, and yet your characters are always in flight from the mundane notions of reality. You write stories not to escape, but to evade the tiresome politics of native victimry. I create traces of totemic creatures, paint visionary characters in magical flight, native scenes in the bright colors of survivance, and you create the same scenes by the tease of words and irony."

Dogroy accounts for his surname as a visionary place, and an actual township on the reservation: "Beaulieu is the place of the visual stories of my art, the shrouds of animals, birds, and visionary figures. Marc Chagall creates visionary scenes over his hometown, Vitebsk, in Russia, on the Pale of Settlement. Beaulieu is my Vitebsk, a settlement on the Pale of the White Earth Nation."[13]

"The books have voices. I hear them in the library," declared Diane Glancy in the first scenes of native poetic motion in *Designs of the Night Sky.* She said, "I know the voices are from the books. Yet I know the old stories do not like books. I hear the books. Not with my ears, but in my imagination. Maybe the voices camp in the library because the written words hold them there. Maybe they are captives with no place to go."[14]

N. Scott Momaday pointed out in *The Way to Rainy Mountain* that his grandmother "lived out her long life in the shadow of Rainy Mountain, the immense landscape of the continental interior lay like memory in her blood." Aho, his grandmother, told stories about the great native migration, a visual journey that continued for some five hundred years. "I wanted to see in reality what she had seen more perfectly in the mind's eye," Momaday wrote.[15] The stories of that memorable native migration and many others are the inadvertent sources of the theory of transmotion or visionary motion, clearly a trace and presence of native continental liberty.

Some trickster stories start with a cursory sense of motion, "Trickster was going along," and the listener or reader can easily sense and imagine the natural motion at the start of the story, and with no declaration of time or character actuation. Maybe some listeners and readers have lost the capacity to appreciate the transmutations of time, gender, water, myths, ironic scenes and the many mutations of trickster figures by gesture, word, imagination, and tricky maneuvers. These trickster gestures create a sense of visionary motion. The stories of native creation and trickster scenes were seldom told in the same way, and visionary characters must elude simulations, description, causation, denouement, and cultural victimry.

The Constitution of the White Earth Nation provides that the "freedom of thought and conscience, academic, artistic irony, and literary expression, shall not be denied, violated or controverted by the government." Probably no other constitution in the world has specifically protected the individual rights of artistic practices, an ironic literary manner, natural motion, and cultural sovereignty.[16]

These constitutional sentiments of ethos, survivance, and liberty are revealed in ancient cave art, sacred objects, the natural motion of animals, and in the obvious creative resistance of modern native painters and literary artists to dominance, and cultural separatism. Native transmotion and survivance are visionary, and the images of motion are painted on the walls of ancient caves, marked on stone, hide, birch bark, paper, and canvas.

Native and indigenous cosmototemic artists created the first memorable scenes of presence, natural totemic motion, and survivance on the slant of stone and in the great shadows of monumental caves more than thirty thousand years ago on every continent. The spirited shadows of cave bears, lions, horses, birds, and elusive shamans dance forever on the contours of the ancient stone.

Shadows are a natural presence in native stories and artistic scenes. Shadows are vital motion, visionary and animate, and create a sense of presence. The Anishinaabe word *agawaatese*, for example, is translated as a shadow of flight, a totemic image of presence, not the mere absence of light, or a passive cast of the source. The traces of shadows are a presence in stories and art.

The Chauvet Cave on the Ardèche River in France is home to one of the most recent discoveries of ancient art. The stately scenes of cave bears, lions, and horses are spectacular, and the shadows and natural motion of the totemic animals are evocative after some thirty thousand years. The singular portrayal of a row of cave horses is similar to the visionary horses painted on hide, paper, and on canvas by native cosmototemic artists.

Carl Beam was an extraordinary visionary and innovative artist. The traces of elemental scenes and modes of transmotion, contour overlays, the ironic union of images, and transparencies are obvious in his elusive creations of manifold portrayals and chronicles. Christopher Columbus, for instance, is pictured on one panel and a common electric meter in another panel, and an elk afloat with bloody handprints. Sitting Bull, in a rouge hue, stands alone in one panel, a posed photograph, and in the other panels the artist portrays a railroad engine and scenes of the dissection of whales. These elements and ironic scenes were imagined in an abstract collage of familiar images, an obscure association of reflections and portrayals.

Beam created a collage of a raven, buffalo, and nude political prisoner that could have been painted in a cave. "Red dots, the celestial decoration on ancient stone, and contours of natural motion portray the shamanic resurrection of a bare and desolate Wichita woman decorated with costume jewelry. William Soule had photographed the woman and other political prisoners at Fort Sill, Oklahoma." The scene creates a sense of survivance with only one posed photograph in a collage of memories by Native Americans. The scene is "forever in motion, a natural resurrection of cave art."[17]

Sacred objects are perceived in transmotion and spiritual transcendence and inspired by the visionary sense of heart and spirit, not by the mundane cultural notice of tradition, provenance, or museum acquisitions. Sacred medicine bundles, for instance, are singular sources of spiritual power that heal the heart and induce by song, music, art, dance, meditation, and astute trickery the vital ethos of transmotion and the spirit of cultural survivance.

The Zuni *Ahayu:da* are war gods, sacred figures that create a sense of spiritual and communal protection in the world. The *Ahayu:da* have been removed and stolen from sacred sites by explorers, anthropologists, traders, and sold to collectors, galleries, and museums. The spiritual essence of visionary motion and an everlasting native presence was appropriated as a commercial artifact.

The Native American Graves Protection and Repatriation Act of 1990 requires institutions, universities, and other agencies that receive money from the federal government to negotiate the return of sacred objects and human remains. Many of the *Ahayu:da* were returned and the natural motion and harmony of the world was restored.

The "Zuni have been more proactive than other Native American Tribes in reclaiming ceremonial objects," reported Rachel Donadio in the *New York Times*. Specifically, more than a hundred *Ahayu:da* have been returned from "institutions and collections in the United States. The Zuni have taken advantage of federal legislation that requires all United States institutions to return objects considered sacred by Native Americans." Those laws, however, "do not apply in Europe." The repatriation of the *Ahayu:da* from Europe is a moral matter, not a legal order.

Octavius Seowtewa, a Zuni elder, told the reporter for the *New York Times* that "if you listen to us about the power these objects have to our community, that these are exemplars of sacred objects," the museum directors would respond favorably. Seowtewa, however, acknowledged recently "that he hadn't had much luck in his meetings at the Musée du Quai Branly" in Paris or the "Ethnological Museum in Berlin."[18]

"Call me Ishmael," an ironic biblical name in the first sentence of the novel *Moby-Dick* by Herman Melville, is one of many first person voices that are overheard in libraries, trickster stories, and in literary adventures. Melville creates a truly memorable sailor of natural motion and spectacular survivance and pursues the ironic visionary and moral transcendence of a crippled sea warrior and transmotion of a mighty white whale.

Ishmael is an everlasting trope and trouble of natural motion and transcendence and the very tease of reality and mortality. "But this deepest fear is not death; he fears that there is nothing beyond our shell of existence; there is no ideal reality beyond the material; there is nothing," observed John Bryant in "*Moby-Dick* as Revolution." Nothingness is a paradox, of course, but it is a "universal constant with no higher reality."[19]

Herman Melville is a master of the tropes of motion, and he creates an essential sense of visionary motion or transmotion in almost every scene of *Moby-Dick*, but his literary mastery and perceptions of natural motion are more direct and descriptive in the chapter "The Tail." He is noticeably more representative than visionary and describes five specific motions of whale tails. The fifth motion is "the ordinary floating posture."[20]

Melville describes the actual motions of the whale tails as knowing and necessary, yet he declares, "The more I consider this mighty tail, the more do I deplore my inability to express it. At times there are gestures in it, which, though they would well grace the hand of many, remain wholly inexplicable." Yes, the natural motion of the whale tails may be "mystical gestures." He concludes the chapter with references to signs and symbols, an ironic conversation "with the world."[21] The cetology and whale tail discourse in this chapter mimic the creative transmotion or the visionary scenes of motion in the novel *Moby-Dick*.

Ishmael related in the first scene of *Moby-Dick* that when he was sidetracked on a dreary day, he paused at "coffin warehouses" and then "quietly took to the ship. There is nothing surprising in this," and "almost all men in their degree, some time or other, cherish very nearly the same feelings towards the ocean with me."[22] That portrayal of the sentiments of the ocean is an obvious invitation to stories of natural motion, and no matter the tease or chance of a whaler, the creases, thrust, and surge of waves, the natural motion of the sea always provides a sublime transcendence of sorrow, separation, cultural closure, and victimry.

"So ignorant are most landsmen of some of the plainest and most palpable wonders of the world," Ishmael declared, "that without some hints touching the plain facts, historical or otherwise, of the fishery, they might scout at Moby Dick as a monstrous fable, or still worse and more deplorable, a hideous and intolerable allegory."[23] The reference to an "intolerable allegory" is a literary gesture that respects the natural motion of the great whale, not the mere parable or moral stories that reveal an obscure and covert sense of absence and literary closure. Moby Dick is a trope of transmotion, and the menace of the mighty white whale outmaneuvers the similes of literary whalers and the missionaries of enlightenment.

Natural motion and transmotion are portrayed in the scenes of the ocean, and sailors in search of whales. Moby Dick, the great white whale, however, is an obscure presence in the novel, and the outcome is not an unbearable or mere nihilistic allegory of vengeance or victimry. Natural motion is a heartbeat, ravens on the wing, the rise of thunderclouds, the surge of ocean waves, and the mysterious weight of whales. Transmotion is the visionary or creative perceptions of the seasons and the visual scenes of motion in art and literature. The literary portrayal and tropes of transmotion are actual and visual images across, beyond, on the other side, or in another place, and with an ironic and visionary sense of presence. The portrayal of motion is not a simulation of absence but rather a creative literary image of motion and presence.

Ishmael related that he would paint "without a canvas something like the true form of the whale" and announced that it was "time to prove that some pictures of whales were wrong. It may be that the primal source of all those pictorial delusions will be found among the oldest" sculptures of the Hindus, Egyptians, and Grecians.[24]

"The French are the lads for painting action," Ishmael declared, and the "natural aptitude of the French for seizing the picturesqueness of things seems to be particularly evinced in what paintings and engravings they have of their whaling scenes. With not one tenth of England's experience in the fishery, and not the thousandths part of that of the Americans, they have nevertheless furnished both nations with the only finished sketches at all capable of conveying the real spirit of the whale hunt."

The French portrayed scenes of whales with a visionary sense that conveyed transmotion and the surge of the ocean. The "English and American whale draughtsmen seem entirely content with presenting the mechanical outline of things, such as the vacant profile of the whale; which, so far as picturesqueness of effect is concerned, is about tantamount to sketching the profile of a pyramid."[25]

The portrayals of whales that Ishmael so admired were in natural motion, visionary images that transcended the closure of a "mechanical outline" and created a sense of the presence of whales. He favored the painterly show of transmotion, the surge of the ocean, and likewise revealed the same sense of motion in narratives.

Moby Dick, the great white whale, is a spectacular portrayal of literary transmotion, a spirited and mysterious image of natural motion in the ocean, in the book, and in the imagination of the reader. "One often hears of writers that rise and swell with their subject," declared Ishmael. "How then, with me, writing of this Leviathan?" The "mere act of penning my thoughts of this Leviathan, they weary me, and make me faint with their outreaching comprehensiveness of sweep, as if to include the whole circle of the sciences, and all the generations of whales, and men, and mastodons, past, present, and to come, with all the revolving panoramas of empire on earth and throughout the whole universe, not excluding its suburbs."[26]

Rightly so, the great portrayals of whales are in natural motion, the scenes of transmotion and "panoramas" of the universe. Likewise, the notable diction of the narrator and his astute manner, gesture, and maneuvers of words created images of natural motion in science, ideologies, and history. Ishmael created a figurative sweep of humans and whales and a distinct sense of natural motion in a narrative of irony and chance.

Stephen Zelnick declared the novel *Moby-Dick* "a mediation on democracy." Consider the scenes of equality in the novel, "the exalted imagery of common workmen." Ishmael "tells us more about the embattled American experience in liberty and democracy than most have chosen to recognize."[27]

Melville created contentious characters in natural motion, and the scenes of visionary transmotion, political ideologies, moral transcendence, and vengeance were carried out in the spectacular pursuit of the constant motion of a mysterious white whale.

John Bryant asserted in "*Moby-Dick* as Revolution" that the novel "depicts the struggle to understand the relation between the promise of transcendental thought and its abnegating opposite, the fear of nothingness." *Moby-Dick*, "at first glance . . . seems a revolution almost exclusively in its aesthetic modernity. The long, rhythmic lines, the prose poetry, the mixture of genres and multiplicity of voices, the experiments in point of view, symbolism, and psychology," however, the "novel's radical politics seem strangely submerged. Surely, we can extract from the novel's veil of allegory a prophetic warning that the American ship of state is heading toward the disaster of Civil War."[28]

The narrative structure, chase of whales, luminous waves, and figurative portrayals of the ocean create a literary sense of natural motion. "Ishmael knows the transcendental problem. He begins in crisis, seeing death," but "his deepest fear is not death; he fears that there is nothing beyond our shell of existence" and the absence of a reality. John Bryant wrote that "Ishmael takes to sea democratically to confront his fear of nothingness, just as Ahab takes to seas autocratically to kill that fear in the form of the white whale."[29]

The Whale by Herman Melville was first published in London in 1851, and later in the same year *Moby-Dick* was published in New York. Melville, once a neglected author, was not widely recognized or celebrated as a literary artist until the end of the First World War. The secure cultural representations of the Enlightenment were in ruins at the time, and the breakdown of rational structures and institutions turned many young survivors into extremists, creative storiers, and innovative artists. *Moby-Dick* was discovered in the context of the ruins of empires, rational governance, and the rise of modern abstract art at the end of the First World War.

Melville created a wild whaler and a direct, expressive narrator of survivance. Ishmael was a sailor portrayed in natural motion, a storier of great ocean waves and exotic scenes of liberty. Ishmael was a sailor of resistance, inspired by chance and transcendence, and he became the sole survivor and storier of the mighty whale Moby Dick, the demise of the tormented and crippled Captain Ahab, and the absolute visionary destruction of the whaleship *Pequod*.

Natural motion and the literature of survivance create a vital and astute sense of presence over absence in stories, art, and literature. "The nature of survivance creates a sense of narrative resistance to absence, literary tragedy, nihility, and victimry. Native survivance is an active sense of presence over historical absence."[30]

Herman Melville clearly conveyed the natural motion of sailors and the sea, and he portrayed the tease, trouble, and havoc of whalers. Ishmael created a sense of presence and situations of transmotion with tropes, diction, character expressions, irony, and comparative scenes. Cosmototemic art and native literary scenes of natural motion and transmotion actuate the world with visionary and ironic stories of cultural survivance. Native totems are personal, ancestral associations with animals and birds, and the necessary metaphors to create a sense of native presence. Natural motion and transmotion are the sources of creative stories, dream songs, and the actual traces of visions scenes in cosmototemic art.

Natives are forever in natural motion with ironic creation stories, and the new literary artists are answerable to the traces of transmotion, that mighty cosmototemic curve of the unnamable in cultural survivance stories.

[4]

Natives of the Progressive Era

Luther Standing Bear and Karl May

The Progressive Era of the late nineteenth century and the early twentieth century was a worldwide chronicle of activism and political simulations, an unreserved succession of cultural notions, institutions, scientific research and practices, and liberal government policies that renounced tyranny, political corruption, racial separatism, poverty, disease, the miseries of industrialization, and the abuses of labor. The cultural sea changes that would advance science, economic systems, technology, public health, politics, music, and the ethos of governance, however, were stark ironies in most rural areas and in native communities. The tributes of progressivism became only the customary tease of the dubious enlightenment on federal reservations for Native American Indians.

Natives were not recognized as citizens of the United States of America, for instance, until the passage of the Indian Citizenship Act in 1924. The Society of American Indians, an association of educated and progressive natives, medical doctors, teachers, authors, and artists lobbied for decades to be recognized as citizens and for other rights that had been denied to Native Americans. The Citizenship Act declared that natives born within the territorial limits of the United States were citizens, and "citizenship shall not in any manner impair or otherwise affect the right of any Indian to tribal or other property."[1]

Natives were mentioned mostly in rumors, stories of racial derision, gossip theories, encounters with the military, and cultural fades in national newspaper stories, and they were slighted in the imagination of newcomers and citizens in urban areas. Natives, the wild outsiders in the pick-and-choose of patois, were honored at times in national reviews. Natives were always relevant to liberal humanists but sidelined in the politics of capricious federal agencies.

Settlers in traditional native territories disregarded treaties, breached the borders of treaty reservations, abused federal policies with impunity, and were envious of native land and resources. Natives were seldom considered as progressive, a stereotype that denied the headway of education and stories of survivance. Poets and fiction writers created simulated natives in marketable stories based on the crude notions of a vanishing race, on cultural hearsay, racial speculation, and the gossip theories and catchwords of ethnography. Most of the scenes in popular literature were fantastic savagery, some nobility, but predictable romantic victimry.

Karl May imagined the marvelous and heroic character Winnetou, an Apache warrior and tribal chief with natural romantic rights, but not as a legal citizen of the United States. The Winnetou novels sold more than a hundred million copies worldwide during the Progressive Era. The first complete translation of *Winnetou* from the original German into English was published about forty years ago, but fragments of the novel were translated in the early 1900s.

May wrote about romantic, heroic natives but never visited a Western reservation, and he apparently never actually attended a Wild West show, but there are rumors that he had met Buffalo Bill. May avoided the shows and natives that toured Germany. He "defamed them as 'outcasts from their tribe' who played 'vile, lying roles,'" declared Rivka Galchen in "Wild West Germany."[2] May was moody about the wild, romantic warriors and traditions he had concocted, and he was rather competitive. Surely the adventure novelist would never consider the spectacle natives as progressive compared to the simulated traditions and natives that traversed his stories. "Meeting travelling Indians might have been awkward for May, especially if he couldn't speak their language," noted Galchen, and it "goes without saying that both Buffalo Bill and Karl May purveyed farragoes of historical misrepresentations."[3] Klara May noted, however, that "Karl was introduced to the Indians and immediately started to speak to them earnestly in a foreign, presumable indigenous language."[4]

Old Shatterhand, the fictional alter ego of the author, related that Winnetou "impressed me deeply from the first sight. I felt that I met an exceptionally intelligent young man, who was equipped with special skills and talent. He also looked at me searchingly with his serious, dark, velvety eyes, which lightened up for a moment as if he was greeting me."[5] Christian Feest pointed out in *Indians and Europe* that the fictional name Winnetou was not gender specific, and a "partial explanation may be found in Arno Schmidt's convincing theory" that the Old Shatterhand and Winnetou "relationship is nothing but a displacement of homoerotic drives."[6]

May "claimed that with Winnetou he had attempted to create an idealized counter-figure to the show Indians who were routinely represented as bloodthirsty," observed Julia Simone Stetler in "Buffalo Bill's Wild West in Germany." Instead, he "wanted to idealize the Indian and make him a romantic symbol." His "opinion about Native Americans was rooted in the German romantic tradition and thus his prototype was not reflected in the arena. . . . May's Indian was born from the Romantic notions of the vanishing Indian that corresponded more with the German image of the Indian off-stage than with the violent one on stage."[7]

Stetler noted that "Karl May festivals are all about smoking the peace pipe, dancing, and powwow style drumming, and not about conflict at all. The Native American image in Germany has always been one of harmony and peace instead of strife and conflict, as it was for Americans."[8] Jan Fleischhauer noted in "The Fantastical World of Cult Novelist Karl May" that May was driven by the "desire to dream his way out of the narrow confines of his real life, a unique mixture of genius and triviality." He was an imposer, the "fictitious persona came naturally," and "because he believed that he was the person he pretended to be, he became convincing to others."[9]

Indian treaties, the obstacles and modern mainstay of native cultures, truly "affected the balance of power within the federal government in ways that created recurring conflict," observed Stuart Banner in *How the Indians Lost Their Land*. Treaties were practical but not progressive because the political convention "committed the federal government to pay tribes in exchange for land cessions." The treaties provided an allocation of money, and the legislature was thereby obligated to "appropriate money" without a choice. Indian treaties and the convoluted federal policies provided an obscure network of dominance, fraudulent intercession, and exploitation of native resources.

Banner explained, "Indian treaties often reserved for Indians the very same land that congressional representatives wanted to grant to settlers, at a time when representatives were the only directly elected members of Congress and many represented districts in which reserving public land for the Indians could be a serious political liability."[10]

The Progressive Era gave rise to territorial strategies that only exploited native reservations by the conversion of communal land to individual allotments provided in the Dawes General Allotment Act of 1887. Native cultures were weakened by separate allotments, and poverty worsened. The new law provided that outsiders could own the treaty land that had not been allotted to natives. The era in this instance was more deceptive than progressive, and a generation later more than half of the native communal land was owned and the resources exploited by speculators.

Karl May published his first Winnetou novel in 1893, three years after the Wounded Knee Massacre on the Pine Ridge Reservation in South Dakota. His romantic novel was beside the point in the traumatic experiences of natives on reservations during the Progressive Era. "The Ghost Dance Movement and the Massacre at Wounded Knee were the subject of extensive newspaper coverage in Germany, and many of the articles were openly critical towards the actions of the American government in this chain of events," noted Stetler.[11]

The public conviction that natives "were the last representatives of a dying race and the witnessing of these discriminatory attitudes moves some German journalists to accuse Buffalo Bill of mistreatments," observed Daniele Florentino in *Indians and Europe*. The "German newspapers had up to then almost ignored the presence" of natives except in the Wild West shows. "German journalists had been more concerned with identifying in the various performances of the Indians the brave deeds of Karl May's heroes," Florentino rightly noted, "than observing the actual performances of the Native Americans."[12]

General Nelson Miles told newspaper reporters in late November 1890, "I go to Washington to confer with the General of the Army concerning the Indian situation. The situation is grave, and the necessity for a vigorous winter campaign is becoming more apparent."[13] Miles described the Massacre at Wounded Knee a month later, December 29, 1890, as a "cruel and unjustifiable massacre." He had written earlier in a telegram to General John Schofield in Washington, "The difficult Indian problem cannot be solved permanently at this end of the line. It requires the fulfillment of Congress of the treaty obligations that the Indians were entreated and coerced into signing." He continued, "Congress has been in session now for several weeks, and could in a single hour confirm the treaty and appropriate the funds for its fulfillment; and, unless the officers of the army can give positive assurance that the Government intends to act in good faith with these people, the loyal element will be diminished, and the hostile element increased." Miles, a progressive humanist in the context of his timely telegram, was at the time commander of the Military Division of the Missouri.[14]

Buffalo Bill, or William Frederick Cody, scheduled Wild West shows in Munich in 1890 and in other German cities the same year as the Massacre at Wounded Knee. The show "featured two hundred cowboys and Indians, Sioux Ghost Dance performances," noted Rivka Galchen, and "reënactments of the battle of Little Bighorn with 'the people who were there!'"[15]

The actual native warriors imitated the battle as a burlesque, a comic variety, and the show was more a wild vaudeville than a historical rendition. The outcome of the show was ironic, an anomaly of slight progress, and hardly a cultural compromise. Natives have always imitated and mocked actual events in stories and enactments, a natural stage of creation adventures, and that included the colonial fur trade.

Progressive notions were underway as hundreds of natives starved, thousands of women and children were undernourished on reservations, and at the same time the arena for the Wild West show in Munich "seated five thousand" and "sold out for each of the eighteen shows."[16] The popularity of the Wild West shows was an ironic declaration of the Progressive Era.

L. G. Moses in *Wild West Shows and the American Indian* observed, "American Horse and Sitting Bull, to name just two Show Indians, found themselves drawn back to their own cultures by their travels with Buffalo Bill. At the same time, other Indians in the shows could discover and then nurture a common 'Indian' identity (as they had done in the Ghost Dance) without weakening tribal ties. It would be wrong therefore to see the show Indians as simply dupes, or pawns, or even victims. It would be better to approach them as persons who earned a fairly good living between the era of the Dawes Act and the Indian New Deal playing themselves, re-enacting a very small portion of their histories, and enjoying it."[17] Clearly, the spectacle or show natives were progressive in the cosmopolitan adventures of Buffalo Bill's Wild West shows.

The Progressive Era was noticeable on reservations only as menace and bleak irony or as evidence of the vicious cutback of the Enlightenment. Charles Eastman, the native medical doctor for the Indian Health Service on the Pine Ridge Indian Agency in South Dakota, treated the few survivors of the Wounded Knee Massacre. Eastman was a progressive and graduate of Knox College, Dartmouth, and the Boston University School of Medicine. He had arrived on the reservation only a few months earlier to practice public health, but instead he served as a battlefield surgeon. Later he was an active member of the progressive Society of American Indians and wrote books that celebrated the courage, honor, and humanity of natives. Eastman and many other natives of his generation, the first to be educated at federal and mission boarding schools, were haunted by the atrocities of the cavalry soldiers at Wounded Knee.

Eastman described the massacre in one of his most notable books, *From the Deep Woods to Civilization*: "At dusk, the Seventh Cavalry returned with their twenty-five dead and I believe thirty-four wounded, most of them by their own comrades, who had encircled the Indians, while few of the latter had guns. A majority of the thirty or more Indians wounded were women and children, including babies in their arms." The wounded were treated at the mission chapel. "We tore out the pews and covered the floor with hay and quilts. There we laid the poor creatures side by side in rows, and the night was devoted to caring for them as best we could." That night heavy snow covered the area, and several miles from "the scene of the massacre," bodies were found buried in the snow. Eastman recalled, "Some of our people discovered relatives or friends among the dead, and there was much wailing and mourning."[18]

Eastman published *Indian Boyhood* in 1902 and *From the Deep Woods to Civilization* in 1916. "I am an Indian," he wrote in the last paragraph, "and while I have learned much from civilization, for which I am grateful, I have never lost my sense of right and justice. I am for development and progress along social and spiritual lines, rather than those of commerce, nationalism, or material efficiency. Nonetheless, so long as I live, I am an American."[19] Clearly, the medical doctor and author was a heartfelt progressive with a sense of ethos and humane governance.

Luther Standing Bear, graduate of the federal Carlisle Indian Industrial School, observed in *My People the Sioux*, "Those soldiers had been sent to protect these men, women and children who had not joined the ghost dancers, but they had shot them down without even a chance to defend themselves. The very people I was following—and getting my people to follow—had no respect for motherhood, old age, or babyhood. Where was all their civilized training?"[20]

Standing Bear was in the first class of native students to attend the experimental school at Carlisle, Pennsylvania, in 1879. He became an educated progressive, returned to the reservation, and taught at the government school for three hundred dollars a year, only to witness a few months later the horror of the Massacre at Wounded Knee Creek.

Standing Bear and many other natives toured with Buffalo Bill's Wild West show in Europe. His participation in the shows as a translator, horseman, and dancer was considered progressive in a sense and, of course, as cultural irony. He received a regular salary and appreciated the experiences and adventures in the world, and surely he perceived the heady onset of marketable du jour simulations and ironic spectacles of great native warriors in staged battles with the cavalry.

Standing Bear had six children with his wife Nellie DeCrory. Alexandra Birmingham Cody Standing Bear was born on June 7, 1902, on tour in Birmingham, England, and Cody was the godfather. Alexandra was named in honor of the queen of England. Three years later, on July 4, 1905, Standing Bear was named the chief of the Oglala Lakota. Then, seven years later, at age forty-four, he was hired by the movie director Thomas Ince and moved to California. He was a progressive member of the Screen Actors Guild, published four books in twenty years, and performed in more than a dozen motion pictures, including *Ramona* in 1916, *The Santa Fe Trail* in 1930, and *Union Pacific* in 1939, the year of his death.

Standing Bear was an intern at John Wanamaker's department store in Philadelphia in 1883 when he read in a newspaper that Sitting Bull was scheduled to lecture to a large audience. The young progressive attended the lecture and was troubled by the false translation. The Lakota leader spoke about peace and admired the great progress of white people, but the translator related only fanciful stories of the warrior Sitting Bull and the massacre of General George Armstrong Custer at the Little Big Horn in June 1876. Later at the hotel, Sitting Bull told Standing Bear, the eager and progressive graduate, "He wanted his children educated in the white man's way, because there was nothing left for the Indian." Standing Bear noticed the translator was in the room so he "did not get a chance to tell Sitting Bull how the white man had lied about him on stage."[21] Sitting Bull was a spiritual healer and a visionary of liberty. He fully resisted dependency on the government, and he was not in the company of warriors that directly attacked the Seventh Cavalry near the Little Big Horn River in Montana.

"Sitting Bull and the Hunkpapa Sioux joined Buffalo Bill's Wild West show in Buffalo, New York," noted L. G. Moses in *Wild West Shows and the Image of the American Indian.* "The 1885 season confirmed the success of Cody's Wild West both financially and artistically. Cody and company toured more than forty cities in the United States and Canada. A part of the show's success is explained by the presence of Sitting Bull."

Natives were separated as detainees on government exclaves or treaty reservations in the late nineteenth century. Native families were weakened by military malice, poverty and starvation, agency corruption, and settler resentment at the time of economic crises. Naturally, natives "accepted one of the few jobs they could find, as entertainers," wrote Moses, and "for much of the twentieth century economic opportunities for Indians rarely broadened and typically centered on their willingness to 'play' Indians. . . . Yet, they found in the Wild West shows a means to evoke and even to celebrate their cultures. 'Playing' Indian would also be viewed as defiance."[22]

The Progressive Era embraced scientific, linguistic, and ethnographic studies of Native American Indians. Natives were the subjects, and at times the casualties of gossip theories, or the new comparative and scientific research of cultural practices. The United States Congress, for instance, established the Bureau of American Ethnology in 1879 to organize an archive of research on the Indians of North America. The government subsidized hundreds of studies that established dominant methods and structures of scientific observations, and these published documents became national endorsements that recorded and revised native cultures, or the vanishing race. The comparative methods of research, or salvage ethnography, evoked racial separatism and manifest differences rather than cultural similarities of temperament, behavior, ethos, and humane principles. The early and most notable researchers included Franz Boas, Frances Densmore, Garrick Mallery, Washington Matthews, and Paul Radin. Public officials, newspaper writers, and novelists consulted the government documents of gossip theories and created a vast narrative of concocted cultures for more than a century. Now, these many studies on music, ceremony, myth, trickster stories, art, games, and languages published in the past century have become a new national archive of steady contradictions and gossip theories that reveal the ethnographic treasure of unintended irony.

"By the end of the first two decades of the nineteenth century, when philanthropy and the churches could show few positive results from their efforts to lift the Indians, doubts were raised about whether they could really be civilized," declared Robert Bieder in *Science Encounters the Indian*. Further, "many such critics began to question the monogenetic assumptions, set in the Bible, that all mankind shared the same origin. Increasingly they began to explain Indians' recalcitrant nature in terms of polygenism. The polygenist Indians were separately created and were an inferior species of man."[23]

The scientific contest of these racial views, the godly monogenetic creation and secular notions of polygenism, an unaccountable and separate creation, has generated a wide range of metaphors and gossip theories about the culture and behavior of contemporary Native Americans. Natives specified as monogenetic in specious scientific theories could be educated, but separate savage creations were not educable. Some politicized the science and argued that natives were separate and primitive and did not deserve education or public support. These views were neither progressive nor traditional. Rather, the racial theories of separatism and later the notions of polygenism were combined with the scientific promotion of eugenics and euthanasia programs, the selected and forced sterilization as government policy in the Progressive Era. Thousands of native women were sterilized without their permission. The most notorious eugenics strategies were carried out in Germany and the United States.

Germany was the first nation to "enact a modern eugenical sterilization law," proclaimed the editors of *Eugenical News* in 1933. However, "Doubtless the legislative and court history of the experimental sterilization law in 27 states of the American union provided the experience which Germany used in writing her national sterilization statute. To one versed in the history of eugenical sterilization in America, the text of the German statute reads almost like the 'American model sterilization law.'"[24]

I directed a progressive desegregation program almost fifty years ago in the Park Rapids Consolidated School near the White Earth Reservation in Minnesota. The elected school board, administrators, and teachers were concerned about the high dropout rate of Native American students compared to other students and determined that natives were culturally deprived on the reservation and did not actually think or reason in the same way as other students. The native students on the reservation, however, had scored above the standards on national examinations, and the scores declined at the consolidated high school. The comparative notion of racial differences in imagination and thought process was a metaphor derived from polygenetic creation, that natives were not created in the same way as other public school students.

The metaphors of racial differences derived from the racial and separatist politics of nineteenth century science are embedded in the ordinary language of contemporary public schoolteachers, elected school board members and administrators. The separatist favors of the early scientific notions of polygenism and monogenesis prevail in the discussion of cultural distinctions, albeit inadvertently and without obvious political objectives. Ethnographic gossip theory and the separatist metaphors and ideologies of single or separate creations were derived from the crude comparative methods of science in the Progressive Era.

The Native American sense of progressive thought, principles, and actuality are probably best articulated by Charles Alexander Eastman in *From the Deep Woods to Civilization*: "The Pine Ridge Indian Agency was a bleak and desolate-looking place in those days, more especially in a November dust storm such as that in which I arrived from Boston to take charge of the medical work on the reservation. In 1890, a 'white doctor' who was also Indian was something of a novelty, and I was afterward informed that there were many and diverse speculations abroad as to my success or failure in this new role, but at the time I was unconscious of an audience. I was thirty-two years of age, but appeared much younger, athletic, and vigorous, and alive with energy and enthusiasm."[25]

5

Expeditions in France

Native Americans in the First World War

Arthur Elm enlisted in the American Expeditionary Forces from Oneida, Wisconsin, and served with a machine gun company in the Thirty-Second Infantry Division. He was wounded in the chest at Cierges, France, and recovered with blood transfusions.

"After this, I didn't know what I was. I was a mixture of Indian, Irish, and Swede," he told the photographer and author Joseph Dixon. Elm told ironic stories in spite of his wounds, situational blood, and empire wars, and he was sensible about service in the military: "It ain't a bad life. Some guys kick about it, but I don't see if they are true Americans why they kick. Army life has got to be hard. You can't make heaven out of it."

Elm returned at the end of the war and "a guy on the boat called out, 'Who wants to re-enlist?' He meant it as an insult to the Army. I felt it was a pretty dirty remark. He didn't appreciate the kind of country he is living in, or the kind of country we have been fighting for."[1]

John Clement Beaulieu, my great uncle, served in an engineer regiment with the American Expeditionary Forces in France. He constructed roads and bridges under enemy fire, and forty years later told me stories about the lovely women he got to know during the Great War. Otto Dix, an expressionist painter, was a soldier in a machine gun unit in the German army. He received an Iron Cross for bravery and later created "unforgiving art" of the First World War. His portrayals of war were "hideous, freakish scenes of human misery and disfigured faces," noted Roberta Smith in the *New York Times*.[2] Otto Dix, in contrast to John Clement Beaulieu, my great uncle, and Arthur Elm, scarcely told stories of romance and certainly did not create ironic stories of France.

"Armistice Signed, End of the War! Berlin Seized by Revolutionists; New Chancellor Begs for Order; Ousted Kaiser Flees to Holland," was the huge banner headline of the *New York Times* on Armistice Day, November 11, 1918. The Treaty of Versailles and the revolutions in Germany and Russia deposed two empire unions and gave rise to political extremism, nationalism, and communism, such as the Nazi Party, the Communist Party, *Action Française* in France, and the National Fascist Party in Italy.

The breakdown of empires and enlightenment, political credibility, cultural unity, and salon aesthetic turned many survivors of the war into extremists, allegorists, and creative storiers. Expressionism, futurism, surrealism, jazz, and cubism generated avant-garde art, music, literature, and an exuberance of cultural conversions, singular visions and experiences, and exotic traces of remembrance. Modris Eksteins observed in "Memory and the Great War" that "André Breton, the surrealist, spoke of the 'crisis of the object.' But, as the ideas of Sigmund Freud suggested, there was a 'crisis of the subject' too. Psychoanalytic theory had a special importance in the search for a new reality."[3]

The native Anishinaabe have endured two empire world wars, the first in the late eighteenth century in North America. "The Ojibways figured in almost every battle which was fought during these bloody wars, on the side of the French against the British," wrote William Warren in the *History of the Ojibway Nation.* The Anishinaabe viewed with sorrow the "final delivery of the Northwestern French forts into the hands of the conquering British." The cultural bonds "which had been so long riveting between the French and Ojibways were not so easily to be broken."[4] Warren was Anishinaabe and published the first reliable history of natives in the late nineteenth century.

Blue Ravens, my historical novel, is the first published narrative about Native American Indians, mostly my relatives from the White Earth Reservation in Minnesota, who served in the American Expeditionary Forces in France. Ignatius Vizenor and his younger brother Lawrence were at home on the White Earth Reservation that Sunday morning, June 28, 1914, when a slight twenty-year-old Bosnian Serb, Gavrilo Princip, shot and killed Archduke Franz Ferdinand and his wife Sophie on a narrow street in Sarajevo.

That obscure assassination carried out more than five thousand miles away was the symbolic start of the First World War, a chance moment of political violence that caused a deadly chain reaction and implicated empires, monarchies, autocratic and egalitarian states, entire continents, the colonial world, and, no less, the Anishinaabe of the White Earth Reservation in northern Minnesota.

The "Great War marked a break in Europe's history," declared Margaret MacMillan in *The War That Ended Peace.* "Before 1914," she argued, "Europe for all its problems had hope that the world was becoming a better place and that human civilization was advancing. After 1918 that faith was no longer possible for Europeans. As they looked back at their lost world before the war, they could feel only a sense of loss and waste."[5]

Corporal Louis Barthas, the French infantry soldier, wrote in his notebook, "If we suffered so stoically, without raising useless complaints, don't let anyone tell you that it was because of patriotism, or to defend the rights of peoples to live their lives, or to end all wars, or other nonsense. It was simply by force, because as victims of an implacable fate we had to undergo our destiny."[6]

John Clement Beaulieu, William Hole in the Day, Ignatius and Lawrence Vizenor, Allen Trotterchaud, Robert Fairbanks, Louis Swan, John Martin Squirrel, and forty other Anishinaabe young men in Becker County on the White Earth Reservation served in the American Expeditionary Forces. Citizens of the White Earth Reservation read some of the gruesome stories of the war, how the *Lusitania* was torpedoed by a German submarine in 1915, about the Battle of Passchendaele and the Somme, and happenings at curious place names in *The Tomahawk*, an independent weekly newspaper published by Augustus Hudon Beaulieu.[7]

General John Pershing, commander in chief of the American Expeditionary Forces in France, lost more than twenty-six thousand "in little more than a month" in the October 1918 offensive at Meuse-Argonne in France, "a carnage far worse than the Civil War battles at Shiloh, Antietam, Gettysburg and Cold Harbor put together." Pershing was fortunate that the "death toll never sank in at home, unlike in Britain after the Somme, thanks to a combination of tight military censorship, embedded reporters who maintained an 'enthusiastic silence' about the body count," and "front-page speculations about the impending armistice."[8]

Private Ignatius Vizenor served in the 118th Regiment of the Thirtieth Infantry Division, and his younger brother, Corporal Lawrence Vizenor, served in the Thirty-Third Infantry Division. Ignatius was killed in action on October 8, 1918, at Montbréhain, France, on the very same day his brother Lawrence Vizenor received the Distinguished Service Cross for bravery in combat at Bois du Fays near Bois de Forêt and Cunel, France.[9]

Private Charles Beaupré, a close friend from the White Earth Reservation, was also killed in action on October 8, 1918, at Saint-Quentin, France. An airplane pilot noted in his diaries that the weather that fateful day was murky, and a cold misty rain covered the devastated countryside.

I visited the same sites of combat at Bony, Montbréhain, Saint-Quentin, and Bois du Fays on October 8, 2011.[10] On the same day of the month almost a hundred years later, the weather was the same, cold and murky, but the landscape was rich, green, and with bright yellow tracks of rapeseed flowers. The traces of bodies and shattered bones of thousands of soldiers were forever harrowed in that gorgeous landscape. Memories of that wicked empire war remained at every turn, crossroad, river, mound, and in the many military cemeteries.

Basile Beaulieu observed in *Blue Ravens*, "There were more American Ford ambulances on the road than motor cars on the entire White Earth Reservation." The wounded soldiers "were on ships at sea, and the dead soldiers, pieces of young bodies, shattered bones, were buried in the earth, some by tillage of mince and morsel, and others by name and poignant ceremonies at military cemeteries. The larger human remains were tagged by religious order, covered and stacked on trucks. The earth would return once more to mustard and sugar beets, and rivers would carry forever the bloody scent of these ancient scenes of war out to the sea."[11]

Representative Julius Kahn of California introduced a resolution shortly after the declaration of war on April 6, 1917, that "called for the immediate organization of 'ten or more regiments of Indian cavalry as part of the military forces of the United States, to be known as the North American Indian Cavalry,'" wrote Thomas Britten in *American Indians in World War I*. The proposed legislation of an "Indian Cavalry" was actually considered by several representatives, and two other measures to segregate native soldiers were introduced by Representative Charles Carter of Oklahoma and Senator Boies Penrose of Pennsylvania.[12]

The "Red Progressives," or the Society of American Indians, and the Indian Rights Association resisted the initiatives to segregate native soldiers. The society argued in favor of integrated units, and pointed out that "segregated units encouraged the maintenance of racial stereotypes, undermined Indian progress, and gave Native Americans an inferior social status."[13] Arthur Parker and Gertrude Bonnin, or Zitkála-Šá, were prominent members of the Society of American Indians, and they "strongly favored the participation of American Indians in the European conflict as a way to demonstrate American Indian patriotism."[14] The secretary of war and several senior military officers ruled against the segregation of Native American Indians in the military.[15]

Wassaja, or Carlos Montezuma, the distinguished Yavapai medical doctor, declared that natives had been mistreated by the government and should not be forced to enlist and fight for the United States. Montezuma argued that the government had no "legitimate authority to require that they perform military service." Matthew Dennis pointed out in *Red, White, and Blue Letter Day*, "Native people served not only in uniform but in striking numbers on the home front as well, with service in the Red Cross and heavy investment in Liberty Bonds."[16]

Native American Indians invested more than $8 million in several initial issues of liberty bonds. By the end of the war, "Native Americans had purchased over 25 million dollars worth of Liberty Bonds, a per capita investment of about 75 dollars" wrote Thomas Britten in *American Indians in World War I*.[17]

Native American soldiers were selected as combat scouts more often than others and served as code talkers but were not segregated as a federal or military policy. The Choctaw, Lakota, Cherokee, Comanche, Osage, Chippewa, or Anishinaabe, Oneida, and other native languages were used to deliver secure military messages by telephone. The Germans were not able to translate the structure, syntax, and metaphors of oral languages. The French had more access to telephone systems in communities.

Russell Barsh pointed out in "American Indians in the Great War" that the "War Department estimated that 17,313 Indians registered for the draft and 6,509, representing roughly 13 percent of all adult Indian men, were inducted. This did not include voluntary enlistment." The Indian Office estimated that "at least half of all Indians who served were volunteers. Total Indian participation was therefore probably 20 to 30 percent of adult Indian men," compared to 15 percent of all adult American men who served in the war.

Barsh estimated that at "least 5 percent of all Indian servicemen died in action, compared to 1 percent for the American Expeditionary Forces as a whole."[18] About 8 percent of the Anishinaabe soldiers from Becker County on the White Earth Reservation were killed in action or died from combat wounds. Britten cited the high casualties and estimated that selected "Indian people suffered even higher casualty rates. The Pawnees, for example, lost 14 percent of their soldiers, and the various Sioux people lost an average of 10 percent. Given their often perilous duties as scouts, snipers, and messengers, the high casualty rate among Native Americans is not surprising."[19]

Only citizens were required by law to register for the draft. Natives "demanded that if the federal government declared they were citizens and thus subject to the draft, they should also be enfranchised." The Bureau of Indian Affairs dithered on the distinction of citizenship and then deviously "turned the entire matter over to the draft boards," observed Thomas Britten. And because they were designed to be flexible and to respond to local needs, the draft boards operated with considerable autonomy."[20]

The Becker County Draft Board on the White Earth Reservation carried out the requirements of the Selective Service Act, the registration of eligible men in the entire county. The total draft "registration for the United States was 23,456,021. Minnesota registered 533,717, and 4,494 of these were from

Becker County." Nearly 15 percent, or 651 men, of the total number registered for the draft in Becker County were selected for military service.

A total of 1,254 men were either drafted or volunteered in Becker County. Fifty-four soldiers in the entire county, or about 4 percent, died in service.[21] That number was four times greater than the number of soldiers who died in the entire American Expeditionary Forces. A total of forty-eight native Anishinaabe soldiers were drafted or volunteered as residents of Becker County on the White Earth Reservation. Four reservation soldiers, or about 8 percent of those who served, died in action in France.

Private William Hole in the Day was born on the White Earth Reservation. He first served in the United States Navy during the Spanish-American War and then in the North Dakota National Guard on the Mexican border. Hole in the Day enlisted in Canada and served in the First Central Ontario Regiment in France. He was poisoned in a gas attack and died on June 4, 1919, at the Canadian General Hospital in Montréal.[22]

Private Ignatius Vizenor was born on the White Earth Reservation. He entered service on February 25, 1918, and served in the 118th Infantry Regiment attached to the British Expeditionary Forces in France. He was killed in action on October 8, 1918, near Montbréhain, France.

Private Charles Beaupré was born on the White Earth Reservation and entered military service on April 22, 1917. He served in the American Tank Corps and was killed in action on October 8, 1918, in Saint-Quentin, France.[23]

Private Fred Casebeer, son of Joseph Casebeer of the White Earth Reservation, served in the 137th Infantry Regiment. He was wounded in action and died on September 30, 1918. Fred Casebeer was buried with more than fourteen thousand other infantry soldiers in the Meuse-Argonne American Cemetery.[24]

Ellanora Beaulieu served as a nurse in the First World War.

She was born May 1, 1889, and died of influenza in service with the army of occupation at a military hospital in Germany. She was buried at Calvary Cemetery on the White Earth Reservation.

The Hindenburg Line was the "greatest challenge" for the soldiers in the Thirtieth Infantry Division. Private Ignatius Vizenor was surely aware that the "casualties were high" in the first offensive. Mitchell Yockelson noted in *Borrowed Soldiers* that "Americans and their allies did not realize . . . that the new attack," early in October 1918, "would mark the beginning of the end of the war."[25]

The commanders of the British Expeditionary Forces ordered the Thirtieth Infantry Division on Tuesday, October 8, to attack and secure an area north of Montbréhain and east of Saint-Quentin, a critical military position in the Hundred Days Offensive. The artillery bombardments had weakened the enemy, but in turns the military strategies were savage and catastrophic to the ordinary way of life in the countryside. The war started with empires, horse parades, and manly military traditions and ended with havoc, enormous tanks and cannons, and new commune cultures of women without men.

The infantry regiment advanced with artillery and heavy tank support early that cold rainy morning, Tuesday, October 8, 1918, sixty-two days into the Hundred Days Offensive. Ignatius was shot in the chest by an enemy machine gun. He caught his breath, collapsed, and died slowly on a cold and muddy ridge near a new series of trenches east of Montbréhain.

Corporal Lawrence Vizenor, Thirty-Third Infantry Division, learned in situations of severe hunger to savor *singe*, or monkey meat, molasses, holey bread, and *pinard*, red country wine, which were standard reserve rations for soldiers in the French army. Corporal Vizenor had already survived combat with the Germans at Château-Thierry, the Second Battle of the Marne, and the Battle of Saint-Mihiel prior to his courageous service in the Meuse-Argonne Offensive.

Robert Ferrell provided in *America's Deadliest Battle* an account of rations for weary soldiers in the Meuse-Argonne Offensive: "Food came up, molasses and French bread with big holes; the molasses trickled on their hands and into their beards, where it mixed with whatever else was there. Dysentery affected everyone, and lack of sleep made them bleary-eyed."[26]

Corporal Vizenor advanced with a platoon of infantry soldiers into the wooded and hilly area of Bois du Fays. "German snipers and machine gunners received no quarter as the doughboys slashed forward through the Bois de Fays," wrote Edward Lengel in *To Conquer Hell*. The patrol encountered intense fire from an enemy machine gun emplacement in the forest. Three soldiers turned back and found cover in a trench. Lawrence, the officer in charge of the patrol, and one other soldier continued to advance on the enemy positions. The officer was wounded in the chest. Corporal Vizenor disabled the machine gun and then carried the officer to a medical aid station.

Corporal Lawrence Vizenor was awarded the Distinguished Service Cross on October 8, 1918, for extraordinary courage and heroism at Bois du Fays in the Bois de Forêt or Argonne Forest.

Nature was hushed, and the shadows of the entire countryside were scenes of wicked rage, bloody, muddy and mutilated bodies stacked for collection at the side of the roads. The elation of the armistice was rightly overcome by the undeniable memories of slaughter, separation, and the inevitable sense of suspicion and vengeance.

Basile Beaulieu wrote in *Blue Ravens*, "The eternal rats tracked down the last dead soldiers and civilians on armistice day to scratch out an eye and chew a tender ear or cold hairy jowl. The native forests and fields would bear forever the blood, brain, and cracked bones in every season of the fruit trees and cultivated sugar beets."

Most of the combat infantry soldiers "returned to small

towns and cities," wrote Beaulieu. Corporal Lawrence Vizenor and other soldiers "returned to a federal occupation on the White Earth Reservation. Our return was neither peace nor the end of the war. The native sense of historical presence on the reservation had always been a casualty of the civil war on native liberty."[27]

6

Visionary Sovereignty

Treaty Reservations and the Occupation of Japan

Thomas Paine boldly declared in the introduction to *Common Sense* at the start of the American Revolution that the "cause of America is in a great measure the cause of all mankind. Many circumstances have, and will arise, which are not local, but universal, and through which the principles of all lovers of mankind are affected, and in the event of which their affections are interested."[1]

Paine later declared in *The American Crisis* about five months before the end of the American Revolution, April 19, 1783, that it was the "cause of America that made me an author." He revealed that his best endeavors were "directed to conciliate the affections, unite the interests, and draw and keep the mind and country together," and "assist in this foundation work of the revolution." Paine worried that the country was in a "dangerous condition," and "the only line that would cement and save her" was a declaration of independence. "I have likewise added something to the reputation of literature," he wrote, "by freely and disinterestedly employing it in the great cause of mankind, and showing that there may be genius without prostitution."[2]

Samson Occom, Joseph Brant, William Apess, George Copway, Black Elk, Charles Eastman, Chief Joseph, Sitting Bull, Luther Standing Bear, White Cloud, William Warren, and many other native diplomats, published authors, and restive storiers worried about the course of racial separatism and might have written that it was the cause of native rights, visionary sovereignty, continental liberty, and peace that made them resistance authors.

"The cause of America is in a great measure the cause of all mankind," Paine wrote in *Common Sense*. "Society is produced by our wants, and government by our wickedness; and former promotes our happiness *positively* by uniting our affections, the latter *negatively* by restraining our vices. The one encourages intercourse, the other creates distinctions. The first is a patron, the last a punishment."[3] Natives were betrayed by the former, the wants of a colonial society, and abused, removed, and murdered by the latter, greedy settlers and constitutional governments. Most of the colonial dominions were not notable sponsors of the rights of natives, and the government incited and at times sanctioned militia atrocities and the military massacre of natives.

Thomas Paine would never "unite the interests" of natives in the revolution, yet he was solicitous at times and denounced natives with unintended irony. He declared the independence of the colonies and then delivered the gossip theories of dominance by comparing the simulation of native revenge and savagery to the crown commanders. Paine wrote in *The American Crisis* 5 that British generals were a "barbarous enemy." General Sir William Howe was "the patron of low and vulgar frauds, the encourager of Indian cruelties; and have imported a cargo of vices blacker than those you pretended to suppress." The "black business" of tortured prisoners and the "history of the most savage Indians does not produce instances exactly of this kind. They, at least, have a formality in their punishments. With them it is the horridness of revenge, but with your army it is the still greater crime, the horridness of diversion."[4]

Paine may have been morose and dour at times, but he never seemed to lose his sentiments of agrarian justice. That sense of justice, however, did not include the rights of natives. "To preserve the benefits of what is called civilized life, and to remedy, at the same time, the evils it has produced, ought to be considered as one of the first objects of reformed legislation."

Paine carried out obvious gossip theories of racial separatism in his narratives, and that left natives in a state of comparative political isolation and cultural absence: "To understand what the state of society ought to be, it is necessary to have some idea of the natural and primitive state of man; such as it is at this day among the Indians of North America. There is not, in that state, any of those spectacles of human misery which poverty and want present to our eyes, in all the towns and streets of Europe. Poverty, therefore, is a thing created by that which is called civilized life. It exists not in the natural state. On the other hand, the natural state is without those advantages which flow from Agriculture, Arts, Science, and Manufactures."

Paine conveyed no understanding of the architecture, arts, agricultural practices, extensive continental trade routes and totemic associations of natives. Yet he declared with unintended irony that the "life of an Indian is a continual holiday, compared with the poor European; and on the other hand, it appears to be abject when compared to the rich. Civilization, therefore, or that which is so called, has operated two ways, to make one part of society more affluent, and the other part more wretched than would have been the lot of either in a natural state."[5]

Some natives at the time might have shared the canons, codes, and cultural ironies of *Common Sense*, the sentiments and conciliated affections of the American Revolution by Thomas Paine. That would have necessitated, however, that colonial pamphleteers were on a "continual holiday."

Samson Occom, William Apess, Joseph Brant, George Copway, and many other natives were tutored at colonial missions. They were the first natives to create a literature of resistance and a sense of survivance in heavy situations of theocratic, colonial, and state coercion. "The outbreak of the American Revolution took many Native Americans by surprise," observed Colin Calloway in *The World Turned Upside Down: Indian Voices from Early America*. Natives in the eastern woodland "held tribal land in common, although individuals had personal property and sometimes kin groups had stronger claims to certain lands," but colonists "insisted on owning the land" that was owned and "excluded by laws and fences."[6]

Natives "made great sacrifices and suffered great losses as result of the American Revolution," noted Calloway, and the misery "represented another step toward the loss of their freedom. At the end of the war, the British and the Americans signed the Peace of Paris, ignoring the Indians who had been their allies and their enemies. Britain handed Indian lands to the United States and left Indian people to confront the renewed American assault on their land and culture." The world was "crumbling around them," and some natives "sought solace in the new religions" and worked with "missionaries and ministers among their own people."[7]

Mohegan Samson Occom, a minister and schoolteacher, published *A Short Narrative of My Life* in 1768. He was critical of colonial dominance and the exploitation of native missionaries by the church:

> I am now to give an Account of my Circumstances and manner of Living. I Dwelt in a Wigwam, a Small Hut with Small Poles and Covered with Matts made of Flags, and I was obligd to remove twice a Year, about 2 miles Distance, by reason of the Scarcity of wood, for in one Neck of Land they Planted their Corn, and in another, they had their wood, and I was obligd to have my Corn carted and my Hay also. . . . Now you See what difference they made between

me and other missionaries; they gave me 180 Pounds for 12 years Service, which they gave for one years Services in another Mission. . . .

So I am *ready* to Say, they have used me thus, because I Can't Influence the Indians so well as other missionaries; but I can assure them I have endeavoured to teach them as well as I know how;—but *I must* Say, "I believe it is because I am a poor Indian." I Can't help that God has made me So; I did not make my self so.[8]

Joseph Brant, the mission educated Mohawk, conveyed a sense of resistance and survivance in his censure of the revolution, and sought to secure the redress of land in his speech before Secretary of State Lord George Germaine in London on March 14, 1776:

Brother, the disturbances in America give great trouble to all our Nations, and many strange stories have been told to us by the people in that country. The Six Nations, who always loved the king, sent a number of their chiefs and warriors with their Superintendent to Canada last summer, when they engaged their allies to join with them in the defense of that country, and when it was invaded by the New England people they alone defeated them.

Brother, in that engagement we had several of our best warriors killed and wounded, and the Indians think it very hard they should have been so deceived by the white people in that country; many returning in great numbers, and no white people supporting the Indians. . . . The Mohawks, our particular nation, have on all occasions shown their zeal and loyalty to the great king, yet they have been very badly treated by his people in that country.[9]

Brant compared British and native Iroquois cultures and remarked, "After every exertion to divest myself of prejudice, I am obliged to give my opinion in favor of my own people."[10]

Samson Occom was one of the first natives to write in English. A *Sermon Preached at the Execution of Moses Paul, An Indian Who Was Executed at New Haven* was published by Thomas and Samuel Green in 1772, several years before the pamphlet *Common Sense* was first published in Philadelphia by Thomas Paine.

"I felt convinced that Christ died for all mankind—that age, sect, color, country, or situation make no difference," wrote William Apess, a Pequot Methodist, in *A Son of the Forest: The Experience of William Apes, A Native of the Forest*, was first published in 1829. Apess, a Pequot missionary, "seems to have been the first Native American to publish his autobiography; he was assuredly the first to create such a substantial body of publications," wrote Barry O'Connell in the introduction to *A Son of the Forest and Other Writings* by William Apess. "Europeans saw their history of print and writing as legitimating their cultural and political dominance. Indians' acquisition of literacy was represented as their acknowledgment of the inferiority of their own cultures, reason enough for many to refuse the opportunity, though from the earliest encounters a significant number did become literate." O'Connell pointed out that to "write as a Native American could then only be an unspeakable contradiction."[11]

Apess wrote that it has been "considered as a trifling thing for the whites to make war on the Indians for the purpose of driving them from their country and taking possession thereof. This was, in their estimation, a right, as it helped to extend the territory and enriched some individuals. But let the thing be changed. Suppose an overwhelming army should march into the United States for the purpose of subduing it and enslaving the citizens; how quick would they fly to arms, gather in multitudes around the tree of liberty, and contend for their rights with the last drop of their blood. And should the enemy succeed, would they not eventually rise and endeavor to regain liberty?"[12]

The Life, Letters and Speeches of Kah-ge-ga-gah-bowh by George Copway was first published in 1847. "The white men have been like the greedy lion, pouncing upon and devouring its prey. They have driven us from our nation, our homes, and possessions," declared Copway. "Is it not well known that the Indians have a generous and magnanimous heart? I feel proud to mention in this connection, the names of a Pocahontas, Massasoit, Skenandoah, Logan, Kusic, Pushmataha, Philip, Tecumseh, Osceola, Patelesharro, and thousands of others. Such names are an honor to the world!"

"And what have we received since, in return?" asked Copway. "Is it for the deeds of a Pocahontas, a Massasoit, and a host of others, that we have been plundered and oppressed, and expelled from the hallowed graves of our ancestors? If help cannot be obtained from England and America, where else can we look? Will you then, lend us a helping hand; and make some amends for past injuries?"[13] Copway, an Ojibwe Methodist, published *The Traditional History and Characteristic Sketches of the Ojibway Nation* in 1851, the first cultural history about the Anishinaabeg in English.

Paine observed in *Common Sense* how "easy is it to abuse truth and language, when men, by habitual wickedness, have learned to set justice at defiance." There is a position, he argued, "not to be controverted, that the earth, in its natural uncultivated state, was, and ever would have continued to be, the COMMON PROPERTY OF THE HUMAN RACE. In that state every man would have been born to property."[14]

Natives, however, were not considered a presence in this natural state. Natives were denied reciprocity and the consummate associations of common property. Paine points out that sovereignty is a "matter of right" that "appertains" to nations but "not to any individual." He declared in the *Rights of Man* that every "citizen is a member of the Sovereignty, and, as such, can acknowledge no personal subjection; and his obedience can be only to the laws."[15]

Chief Joseph, the native diplomat, visited Washington DC in January 1879, two years after surrender in the Bear Paw Mountains, Montana, to argue for tribal recognition and the return of the exiled Nez Perce to their homeland in the Pacific Northwest. Members of Congress, the cabinet, diplomats, and commercial leaders listened to a memorable, heartfelt entreaty for liberty.

Chief Joseph heard a standing ovation at the end of his speech, a version of which was published as an article a few months later in the *North American Review*:

> Treat all men alike. Give them all the same law. Give them all an even chance to live and grow. All men were made by the same Great Spirit Chief. They are all brothers. The earth is the mother of all people, and all people should have equal rights upon it. You might as well expect the rivers to run backward as that any man who was born a free man should be contented penned up and denied liberty to go where he pleases.
>
> When I think of our condition my heart is heavy. I see men of my race treated as outlaws and driven from country to country, or shot down like animals. I know that my race must change. We cannot hold our own with the white men as we are. We only ask an even chance to live as other men live. We ask to be recognized as men. We ask that the same law shall work on all men.
>
> Whenever the white man treats the Indian as they treat each other, then we shall have no more wars. We shall be all alike—brothers of one father and one mother, with one sky above us and one country around us, and one government for all.[16]

These associated tropes, totemic associations, and allegories on the politics of native experience, the diverse causes of resistance, natural reason, survivance, and theories of native sovereignty in a constitutional democracy are thematic, scriptural, and chancy dialogic circles. The gossip theories of clerical and cultural dominance are the inevitable narratives of dominion in the dubious renditions of native rights and cultural liberty.

The native sense of concurrent sovereignty is political and judicatory, of course, and native ancestral sovereignty is a sense of motion, the reciprocity of natural motion, or transmotion, a sense of spiritual or visionary sovereignty. The stories of transmotion are mythic, totemic, and diverse creations. Visionary sovereignty is an association of totems, natural reason, and the politics of families, not the metes and bounds of territorial dominance, monarchial authority, or the mere possession and legal boundaries of property.

The dialogical themes, gossip theories, and course of historical sovereigns and dominion are not easily compared to native reason, transmotion, resistance, the consequences of greedy discovery, and removal of natives to reservations. These distinctions were not perceived or related in the ruins of representation and a constitutional democracy.

The concepts, notions, discourse, and common practices of occidental sovereignty have dominated the cultural, political, and legal histories of natives. The modernist notion of modified domestic, dependent sovereignty, or "limited sovereignty," for instance, a legal contradiction, is a connotation of sovereignty that serves the dominance of discovery and national policies. The current discourse on native sovereignty was first activated in the diverse diction of treaties and has continued in landmark court decisions for more than a century.

"That Indian sovereignty is expressly secured by treaty is no bar to subsequent congressional defeasance," observed T. Alexander Aleinikoff in *Semblances of Sovereignty: The Constitution, the State, and American Citizenship.* Congress, most egregiously, "remains free to abrogate treaty rights and structures unilaterally even in violation of a provision requiring tribal consent for such actions."[17]

The dialogic circles of native sovereignty must now embrace

oral stories, visual and literary memories, and imagistic expressions of native artists and authors. The hundreds of federal treaties negotiated with natives were elusive executive initiatives, and spurious constitutional, legislative compromises that secured extensive native territories with tricky narratives and promises; however, the treaties bear the eternal scriptural traces of government intentions and native transmotion or visionary sovereignty. The treaties, once concessions and evacuation narratives, are now documents of native presence, the oral and scriptural stories of transmotion, and traces of inherent native rights, or an ancestral visionary sovereignty.

John Boli argued in *Problematic Sovereignty*, edited by Stephen Krasner, that the "essence of sovereign" is "theoretical, not empirical; it is the theory that the national polity, as organized by the state, is the pinnacle of authority, neither subordinate to the world polity nor defied by local polities or organizations." Native sovereignty, then, is theoretical and visionary, not subordinate to "world polity" or to local politics and federal policies. "For several centuries, sovereignty has been considered an attribute of states. The state is the locus of ultimate authority in society, uniquely qualified to represent society as a whole in its relations with the external world." Consequently, the "political theory of state sovereignty derived from the ultimate authority of 'the people' is likely to remain well entrenched for many decades to come, though it will also remain disputed, questioned, and, no doubt, much misunderstood."[18]

These discussions of native sovereignty are carried out in two distinct contexts: the first, a sense of native presence, the virtual and actual presence of natives on the continent; and the second, a modernist, comparative discussion of treaties, evacuations, removals, wars, colonial dominance, occupation, and the adventures of legal standing and democratic governance.

The dialogical themes and comparative discussions of native visionary sovereignty focus on virtual cartography, the imagistic expressions of native storiers: visual memories in art, oral stories, native mappery, and literature. Consider, for instance, the images on stone, bark, and hide, totemic and ancestral associations, and natural reason, or the mutual bonds of natives, animals, and nature as totemic sources of visionary sovereignty.

The discussions of modernism or the rational, national conceits of dominance and ethos of democratic governance should consider the contradictions of the political occupation and assimilation and many other capricious policies of the United States of America. Specifically, consider the establishment of native constitutions and representative governments on federal treaty reservations and in occupied postwar Japan.

John Collier, commissioner of Indian affairs in the administration of President Franklin Delano Roosevelt, initiated reform and "recovery" policies through the controversial Indian Reorganization Act. Consider on the one hand the liberal cultural nostalgia of the compromise legislation to "recover" native communities through limited representative governments and on the other hand the unexpected resistance of many natives to the proposed recovery of tribal traditions on reservations. The federal "recovery" of traditions, for some natives, was nothing more than a disguised conformation of dominance and tyranny.

First, natives endured discovery, the cruelties of colonial occupation, and mission separatism, and then they were evacuated to federal treaty exclaves. Subsequently, in the federal course of modernism and assimilation policies, native children were removed to federal boarding schools. Shortly thereafter, native communal treaty land was divided and reduced to individual allotments by the enactment of the Dawes Severalty Act.

Collier, a political activist and social reformer, initiated policies to restore and preserve native cultures, arts, and traditional practices. The policies were based in part on simulated contrition and cultural nostalgia, to restore native traditions and communities by reversals of federal policies and legislation. Congressional resolutions, however, clearly promoted assimilation and dominance; the compromises and corruption incited abuses of natives, sponsored racialist detractions, cultural simulations and gossip theories, and notions of a vanishing race, the very absence of natives.

Collier was the architect of the proposed policy reversal and cultural amelioration, the Weller-Howard Indian Reorganization Act. The legislation provided not only the end of the "long, painful, futile effort to speed up the normal rate of Indian assimilation by individualizing tribal land and other capital assets, but it also endeavors to provide the means, statutory and financial, to repair as far as possible, the incalculable damage done by the allotment policy and its corollaries."[19] Congress, however, had postponed a vote on the appropriations, and the policy was not immediately enacted.

Collier declared in *Indians of the Americas* that the new policy "contained a requirement that every tribe should accept or reject it in a referendum held by secret ballot."[20] The new policy was complicated by time, place, and native practices; the principles of the revisions and proposed cultural ameliorations were not easy to enact in native communities on federal exclaves or reservations. Many natives had been "removed" to reservations from discrete tribal associations and communities.

Francis Paul Prucha pointed out in *The Indians in American Society* that natives, "many of whom were already deeply involved in an individualistic society with their private property and who participated in white governmental procedures, were hesitant about accepting this new plan emanating from Washington." The "return to tribalism" soon became controversial, and questions were raised about the wisdom of the policy.

The Indian Reorganization Act "had major flaws. In the first place, Collier's deepest personal experience with Indians was with the Pueblos of the Southwest, the Indian communities that had been least affected" by the dominant culture. The continuation or return to "tribal ways was possible with them because so much still existed. But for many other tribes

Visionary Sovereignty

the incursion of assimilationist forces had gone too far to be reversed, and acculturated Indians refused to accept Collier's invitation to turn the clock back," observed Prucha; "more damaging is the accusation that an alien form of tribal government was imposed on the tribes by the constitutions adopted under the Indian Reorganization Act."[21]

Collier advocated the recovery of native cultures and a return to the notions of tribalism, while General Douglas MacArthur, supreme commander of the Allied Powers in occupied Japan, established a constitutional government that provided a division of power, elected representation, right of women to vote, right of labor unions to organize, and comprehensive land reform in the postwar ruins of a feudal monarchy.

MacArthur, by his absolute command and occupational interdictions, moved against the traditional authority of the *zaibatsu*, or industrial monopolies, and the imperial monarchy. Military occupations and executive warrants of social and cultural reforms are never the same, but to compare canons of recovery a generation earlier, natives, once evacuated by assimilation policies, were summoned at the very start of modernism to return to their traditions.

"I was thoroughly familiar with Japanese administration, its weaknesses and its strengths, and felt the reforms I contemplated were those which would bring Japan abreast of modern progressive thought and action," MacArthur declared in *Reminiscences: General of the Army Douglas MacArthur*. "First destroy the military power," he wrote. "Punish war criminals. Build the structure of representative government. Modernize the constitution. Hold free elections. Enfranchise the women. Release the political prisoners. Liberate the farmers. Establish a free labor movement. Encourage a free economy. Abolish police oppression. Develop a free and responsible press. Liberalize education. Decentralize the political power. Separate church from state."[22]

General MacArthur should have occupied postwar federal exclaves and reservations in America. His military manner, political bearing, poses of authority, worldly experience, and humane occupation policies were needed on native reservations. The dramatic irony is intended and irresistible in this comparative soliloquy, that free elections, the rights of women, labor movements, a free press, land reform, and much more could be established on reservations, and moreover, that some federal agents might be prosecuted for fraud and corruption and, in some instances, indicted for the incitement of genocide and crimes against peace and tried as war criminals.

John Collier was no Douglas MacArthur.

The Tokyo War Crimes Tribunal prosecuted military leaders for crimes against peace and humanity, and the absolute power of the monarchy was changed forever. The military occupation of the country ended the empire stature of divine rights and established a constitutional democracy. The momentous reversal of Japanese imperialism was not speculative or comparable to the outcome of separatism, wanton violence, and the removal of natives to political reservations in the United States.

The treaties, policies of assimilation, and bureaucratic land allotment legislation were miscarried by corrupt federal agents on native reservations, and at about the same time a modern democratic constitution ended feudalism in favor of land reform and provided a new ethos of individual rights in occupied Japan. Japan has maintained a democratic constitution and government while native communities continue to recover from racial separatism, federal dominance, malfeasance, corruption, and blood quantum politics. Reservation natives were denied basic civil rights in a constitutional democracy and were then summoned to consider policies of nostalgia.

John Collier was sentimental about the revival of native traditions and proposed that natives embrace anew, with fantasies of amelioration, the very traditions that were once denigrated by the military commanders, missionaries, and federal agents. The constitutional provisions of land reform and labor unions were observed for the first time in Japan, yet native communal land was reduced to allotments on treaty exclaves and reservations. Clearly the allotment act favored assimilation and the exploitation of natural resources, but not civil rights and liberty. The crimes of federal agents on reservations were not comparable to enlightened occupation mandates of the constitutional recovery of Japan.

The military occupation of Japan and the duplicitous federal policies of native assimilation and land allotment were not in the same league of governance. The military defeat and occupation of an imperial empire ended with a democratic constitution, but the military and churchy conquest of native cultures turned to gossip theories and the racial documents of separatism.

Consider, though, a wider and thicker comparative critique of the crimes against natives and the responses of military commanders at Sugar Point and Bear Island in Minnesota, the massacres of natives at Sand Creek in Colorado and Wounded Knee in South Dakota, the massacres at My Lai, Vietnam, and Haditha, Iraq. A wider critical discussion and assessment should compare the military occupation and investment strategies of recovery, trade, and economic development policies on treaty reservations to the democratic constitution established in Japan by General Douglas MacArthur, supreme commander of the Allied Powers.

7

Cosmototemic Art

Natural Motion in Totemic and Visionary Art

N ative liberty, natural motion, and survivance are concepts that originated in cosmototemic stories and artistic scenes and in totemic unions that resisted academic
methods, the manner of museum curators, curse of gossip theories, and the deadly policies on federal reservations.

Native survivance is contrary to cultural and political dominance. Survivance creates a sense of native presence and resistance to the sentiments of tragedy. The common suffix of the
two words denotes a distinctive condition and action, and
clearly the outcome is antithetical. Dominant institutions
have sanctioned the absence of natives in history, and publishers have promoted the bankable legacy of victimry. Constitutional democracies are about rights and property, security
and governance, but not always about the ethos of survivance
and artistic liberty.

The Constitution of the White Earth Nation provides that
the "freedom of thought and conscience, academic, artistic
irony, and literary expression, shall not be denied, violated or
controverted by the government." Probably no other constitution in the world has specifically protected the rights of artistic practices and cultural sovereignty.

The preamble to the constitution declares, "The Anishinaabeg of the White Earth Nation are the successors of a great tradition of continental liberty, a native constitution of families, and totemic associations. The Anishinaabeg create stories of natural reason, of courage, loyalty, humor, spiritual inspiration, survivance, reciprocal altruism, and cultural sovereignty."[1]

These constitutional sentiments and ethos of survivance and continental liberty are revealed in ancient cave art, in the natural motion of animals and birds, and in the creative resistance of modern native and indigenous painters to dominance, separatism, and curatorial exclusion of abstract and innovative art. The essential scenes and traces of survivance are visionary and embodied in ancient caves, on stone, hide, birch bark, paper, and on canvas.

The ancient visionary artists painted the first elusive totemic scenes en plein air on granite and sandstone and in atelier caverns that have become in the past century the great museums of cosmototemic art. The artists created a memorable sense of native presence and natural motion by sunlight on stone and by the shimmer of torchlight in thousands of caves on every continent in the world. The unnamed artists and the spirited shadows of cave bears, lions, horses, birds, and elusive shamans dance forever on the contours of the stone. The cosmototemic shadows and natural motion of light have endured for centuries and have inspired modern native and other artists.

Shadows are a natural presence in native perception, a silent remembrance in oral stories and artistic scenes. Shadows are vital, animate, both subject and object, and a presence without a discrete source. The tease of shadows in native stories and painted scenes give rise to the theory of transmotion, an inspired evolution of natural motion, survivance, and memory over time, and a sense of visionary sovereignty. The word *agawaatese*, for instance, in the language of the Anishinaabe, Ojibwe, or Chippewa, is defined as a shadow of flight, and that gesture becomes a significant metaphor of presence in songs and stories. Cosmototemic shadows and scenes created a sense of presence and became the traces of natural motion and survivance. Shadows are totemic, not the mere absence of light or separation by time and circumstances.

Early native artists and indigenous cavern painters were dedicated to the aesthetics of natural motion, the spirited presence of animals, and shamanic visions in abstract shapes, shadows, and patterns. The artistic scenes continued in situ for thousands of years, and once discovered the monumental art has been protected by state governments. The Chauvet Cave is one of the most recent discoveries of ancient native art on the river Ardèche at Pont-d'Arc in France.[2] The stately scenes of cave bears, lions, and horses are spectacular, and the shadows and natural motion of the animals are evocative after some thirty thousand years.[3]

More than thirty species of animals were painted on the natural curves of the cavern, including cosmototemic panthers, owls, and red cave bears. The panels of four horses and nine lions were painted in double motion, from left to right, and with no frame or limit of dimensions. The four heads of the horses are distinctive, painted in a row in natural motion, and the bodies of the animals float on the stone contours of the cavern. The contours of lions were painted in natural motion on the curved stone of the cave. David Whitley observed that at "Lascaux, the animals move away from you in fury; at Chauvet, they come to you in a stately and unhurried pace."[4] The cave scene of the marvelous row of four horses seemed to anticipate the perspective and natural motion of many red, green, and blue horses painted by the untutored native ledger artists who were detained as political prisoners in Fort Marion, Florida.

The Chauvet Cave and Lascaux Cave in France and the Cave of Altamira in Spain are prominent in Europe. The ancient rock art sites in Arizona, California, Minnesota, and Ontario, Canada, are the most famous in North America. There are many other prominent rock art sites in the world. The Cave of Swimmers, for instance, a site of exotic rock art figures in natural motion, buoyant in space on the sandstone, was documented in the mountains of southwest Egypt. Likewise, the Tassili n'Ajjer, located in the Sahara Desert of Algeria, is a site of rock art scenes of hunters with bows, animals, dancers, and other figures. The United Nations Educational, Scientific, and Cultural Organization named Tassili n'Ajjer a World Heritage site.

The Nazca Lines in Peru of an ancient bird in motion, a giant geoglyph, and the enormous wingspan, only fully visible by satellite or drone photographs, are a spectacular scene of visionary motion, or the ancient creation of a magic image scratched on the earth with a perspective and vision of a distance in space. The San Bushmen of Southern Africa painted dancers in motion, floating figures, handprints of presence in caves, shelters, and on the face of rocks and a marvelous scene of two horses in flight with a chariot. Spectacular ancient rock art scenes of extinct animals, intricate and transparent spiritual figures, were revealed and preserved in the Kakadu National Park and the Arnhem Land in Australia. There are more than three hundred caves with ancient indigenous rock art in Spain and France, and thousands more caves of cosmototemic rock art scenes of natural motion on every continent in the world.

Ekkehart Malotki, a linguist, has studied and photographed thousands of ancient rock paintings in Arizona. Malotki and other scholars have considered some ancient rock art as an association of survival. Most academic interpretations of rock art are more descriptive and comparative by line and design than the aesthetic concepts of natural motion and cosmototemic survivance. The actual ancient rock art scenes were visionary, ceremonial, and artistic elements of natural motion and survivance.[5]

The theories of survivance are elusive, obscure, and imprecise as retrospective interpretations of ancient native art, but survivance is invariably necessary, true, and just in native practices of art and stories and in the natural motion of painted scenes on stones and in caves. The nature of survivance is unmistakable in native reason and remembrance, observable in trickster stories and the humanistic tease, or vital irony, and manifest in the spirited resistance to archival, museum, and cultural dominance. The character of survivance creates a sense of native presence and actuality over academic gossip theories, historical separation and absence, nihility, and the romantic sentiments of victimry.[6]

Selwyn Dewdney and Kenneth Kidd studied the ancient rock paintings of shamans, animals in natural motion, totemic cranes, winged figures, serpents, miniature creatures, and handprints near Lake Superior, Lake of the Woods, Lake Missinaibi, and Quetico Provincial Park in Ontario, Canada. These great granite galleries of rock art are cosmototemic, and the scenes are similar to the actual images scored on traditional birch bark scrolls of the Anishinaabeg. The rock images were mostly red ocher and painted with a cedar brush or finger. Dewdney pointed out that the "aboriginal artist was groping toward the expression of the magical aspect of his life, rather than taking pleasure in the world of form around him. Essentially, however, the origin and purpose of these deceptively simple paintings remain a mystery."[7]

Franz Boas, the distinguished anthropologist, closely studied the elements of formalism, representation, and symbolism in the native arts of the Northwest Coast of North America. His integrated ethnographic interpretations were original and learned, to be sure, yet his comparative and taxonomic observations were weighted by academic assignments of "primitive art" and cultures.

Boas observed in *Primitive Art* that representative art "does not affect us by its form alone, but also, sometimes even primarily, by its content. The combination of form and content gives to representational art an emotional value entirely apart from the purely formal esthetic effect." He pointed out, in the context of symbolism, that two elements are distinguished in primitive art, "a purely formal one in which enjoyment is based on form alone, and another one in which the form is filled with meaning."[8]

Form and dimensions are elements of conventional art, and form is customarily defined and framed to show the appearance of depth, the familiar representation of cultural distance. The formal dimensions of representations were determined by traditional painterly practices and by the dominance of art histories.

Ancient artists created visionary forms, cosmototemic scenes, shadows, and abstract patterns and dimensions that were inspired by natural motion, and with traces of cultural memory. The trace and contours of animals and other buoyant figures were painted on stone in more than two or three dimensions, and some scenes were transparent and painted over other original portrayals. The elements of form, perspectives of natural motion, and visionary dimensions in ancient native art anticipated impressionism, cubism, surrealism, and the curious fades of formal portraiture, representation, and modernism.

"Form, in the narrow sense, is nothing but the separating line between surfaces of colour," declared the painter Wassily Kandinsky in *Concerning the Spiritual in Art*. "That is its outer meaning. But it has also an inner meaning, of varying intensity, and, properly speaking, *form is the outward expression of this inner meaning*." Cosmototemic animals, figures, and other forms in natural motion were enhanced by transparency, contours, and the buoyant colors of memory.[9]

Henri Bergson observed in *Creative Evolution* that life and ideas should manifest a "greater harmony" if life, and art in this instance, created "something other than a series of adaptations" to chance circumstances. "If, on the contrary, the unity of life is to be found solely in the impetus that pushes it along the road of time, the harmony is not in front, but behind. The unity is derived from a *vis a tergo*: it is given at the start as an impulsion, not placed at the end as an attraction."[10]

Cosmototemic art is a continuous aesthetic, native scenes of presence, a visionary cruise of natural motion, and the totemic harmony is derived from the actual visionary motion, a wave or stimulation from behind, not the end, a momentary denouement, or the modern sway of transient closures in calendar time.

The ancient artists have inspired avant-garde painters with the vitality of artistic moods, totemic harmony, and the abstract expressions of natural motion. Museum curators, art historians, and some anthropologists once related a complicated succession of art movements on the "road of time," or the curatorial dominance of representations, stages, and artistic eras suitable for museums. The origins and elements of art forms were considered at the same time as the controversial end of curatorial favors, cultural manners, representations, and modernism.

Salons and museums were seldom the centers of innovative art, creative perception of shadows and angles, or the inspiration of natural motion. The distance between the creative episodes of natural motion and cultural representations were never a crisis in the shamanic scenes on rock art or in the untutored portrayals of horses in natural motion by cosmototemic cave artists.

Some form of ancient cosmototemic art exists on every continent of the world, "but the story of art as a continuous effort does not begin in the caves of southern France or among the North American Indians. . . . There is no direct tradition that links these strange beginnings with our own days, but there is a direct tradition, handed down from master to pupil," Ernst Gombrich declared in *The Story of Art*.[11]

Gombrich was rather romantic about the master teachers, but later he conceded that Paul Cézanne, Vincent Van Gogh, and Paul Gauguin had studied and worked "with little hope of ever being understood" as painters.[12] There are no direct traditions or evolutions of art, of course, but the scenes of natural motion and elements of visionary artistic scenes are cosmototemic connections between some ancient rock art and innovative native painters.

"There are only artists," not a definitive art, noted Gombrich: "Once there were men who took coloured earth and roughed out forms of a bison on the wall of a cave; today some buy their paints, and design posters for hoardings; they did and do many other things," and there "is no harm in calling all these activities art."[13] The dominant masters of art practices and traditions once connected only the basic elements of painterly dimensions and cultural separatism and either slighted native artist with academic gossip theories or museum curators lectured on the worth and wonder of untutored art as primitive, the lowest level of artistic representations.

The ancient artists who painted the panel of four horses and other visionary panels of animals on contours of stone at Chauvet Cave and on granite covers in the canoe country near Lake of the Woods are the ancestors of modern native painters of continental liberty. Contemporary cosmototemic artists have created similar scenes of natural motion, horses afloat, and transparent animals in the collage of ancestral remembrance and survivance.

The scenes and shadows of natural motion have inspired artists for centuries, and modern native artists circumvented the curatorial resistance to abstract and expressionist art. Oscar Howe, George Morrison, Robert Houle, Fritz Scholder, Carl Beam, Jaune Quick-to-See Smith, Norval Morrisseau, and Rick Bartow, to name only eight of hundreds of outstanding native artists who have created scenes of transmotion with conceptual contours, temper of colors, and original abstract forms, patterns, and customs.

Some museum curators once deployed a narrow notion of traditional native art practices and excluded several painters from native art exhibitions because they were considered modernists or expressionists and did not paint traditional themes.

The abstract portrayals by Oscar Howe, George Morrison, and other native and indigenous abstract artists were separated and rejected by romantic curatorial doctrines.

Oscar Howe was born almost a century ago on the Crow Creek Reservation in South Dakota. He graduated from the Pierre Indian School during the Great Depression and continued his studies at the Studio School at the Santa Fe Indian School with Dorothy Dunn. Howe served as a combat infantry soldier during the Second World War and later graduated with a master of fine arts from the University of Oklahoma. He was an innovative painter, inspired by abstract art and cubism. In 1958 Howe entered the Annual Painting Competition at the Philbrook Museum of Art in Tulsa, Oklahoma. His abstract entry was rejected because it was considered not to be "traditional" art by an Indian.

"Whoever said that my paintings are not in the traditional Indian style has poor knowledge of Indian art indeed," Howe wrote to the curator of the Philbrook Museum. "There is much more to Indian art than pretty, stylized pictures. There was also power and strength and individualism. . . . Indian art can compete with any Art in the world, but not as a suppressed Art."[14]

The curator had rejected an innovative and abstract painting that was inspired by native traditional designs and by a curious continuation of natural motion and other elements common in cave art. Howe was surely an early cosmototemic painter and much more, and his resistance to curatorial dominance was precise, true, and lasting. He is now celebrated in museums as a visionary abstract painter, not merely as an academic artist of traditional themes. The curator who excluded his abstract art was romantic, protective of the gossip theories of separatist "traditions," and probably either forgiven or forgotten in the history of native art.

The curator who once rejected the original abstract paintings of Oscar Howe was apparently not aware of the abstract geometric patterns on parfleche, or rawhide saddlebags, and other containers created by natives on the Great Plains. Native women painted the functional parfleche containers, a traditional artistic practice.

George Morrison was born on the Grand Portage Reservation in Minnesota. He studied fine art at the Minneapolis School of Art, and the Art Student League in New York City. He was inspired by the art movements of the time, expressionism, cubism, and surrealism, and encountered Jackson Pollock, Franz Kline, and Willem de Kooning at the Cedar Street Tavern in Greenwich Village.

Morrison became a famous international expressionist painter, but museum and exhibition curators would not accept his bold abstract paintings in native art exhibitions for many years because the elements of his style were not considered to be "Indian." Morrison was a brilliant expressionist painter, and he was exhibited among the most distinguished abstract artists in New York City and Europe. The romantic and preservative notions of curators at the time selected art that depicted "traditional" themes or naturalistic scenes that represented gossip theories about native culture, scenes that most viewers would recognize immediately, but not native visionary scenes of abstract expressionism. The curators were misguided, of course, and innovative and abstract portrayals by native artists were seldom embraced by museums until the 1960s.[15]

Morrison teased the elusive colors of natural motion and envisioned an eternal horizon in his memorable abstract creations, an aesthetic meditation on the hues of nature and memory. He learned the words of motion, shadows, and the colors of natural scenes in two languages, one oral and the other written. The Anishinaabe word *inaazo*, an animate verb that means "colored in a certain way," traces the native sensibilities of his expressionistic art. The word *misko*, or "red," for instance, is a visual memory, as in *miskomin*, or "raspberry," *miskwaawaak*, or "red cedar," *miskwi*, or "blood," and *miskwazhe*, "to have measles."

Cosmototemic Art

Morrison likely observed the tricky tone of *ozhaawashko*, a word that means blue and green, the memorable hue of a bruise, or *ozhaawashko aniibiish*, "green tea." The horizons he painted were visionary; the colors and contours were traces of natural motion. The horizon lines were visceral unions of natural motion, a cosmototemic association of stories and memories of sunrises and sunsets. "I believe in going back to the magic of the earth and the lake, the sky and the universe," he declared. "That kind of magic . . . a religion of the rocks, the lake, the water, the sky."[16] George Morrison at the end of his career as a painter lived on the shore of Lake Superior near the Grand Portage Reservation in Minnesota.

The Anishinaabe words *odoodemi*, "to have a totem," and *indoodem*, "my totem, my clan," are an association of natural motion, a sense of totemic presence and survivance, and native resistance to the perversions of power over nature. Totems and natural motion are at the heart of artistic perception and cultural memory.

Dorothy Dunn established the Studio School at the Santa Fe Indian School in 1932. Native artists, she declared, should not be distracted by modernism or any other art movements and should rather concentrate on flat contours that depicted traditional cultural scenes, not knowing that the right to simulate, enact, and represent certain ceremonies was seldom granted by healers and spiritual leaders. "Dunn believed that there was an 'authentic Indian' way to paint," observed Janet Berlo and Ruth Phillips, and "she encouraged the students to derive their inspiration from the great artistic traditions that were their heritage."[17]

Fritz Scholder arrived at the Santa Fe Indian School in the early 1960s and overturned the declared art methods of Dorothy Dunn. He changed the "traditional" style to abstract expressionism and cubist figurations. "The single most important institutional force in the development of modernist native art was the Institute of American Indian Arts in Santa Fe," declared Berlo and Phillips. Scholder was among the most "influential teachers, inculcating ideas of individual artistic freedom, and training many of the most notable American and Canadian Native artists" for more than a generation.[18]

Jaune Quick-to-See Smith, a descendant of the Salish and Kootenai in Montana, has created marvelous abstract paintings of figures, petroglyphs, landscapes, transparent silhouettes, and bold layers of images, contours, exotic mappery, erasures, and ironic slogans and concepts of popular culture. The lithograph *Solar, Sacred and Secular* shows a horned buffalo skull divided by bold abstract colors, painted over the black and white simulation of fifteen wooden wire spring clothespins.

Solar, Sacred and Secular and more than a dozen other paintings were included in *Plains Indians: Art of Earth and Sky*, an exhibition in the Flomenhaft Gallery at the Metropolitan Museum of Art. *The Trade Canoe: Don Quixote in Sumeria* is a spectacular abstract canoe loaded over the gunwales with human skulls, body parts, and a cowboy skeleton riding the bare bones of a horse. The canvas is huge, five feet high and more than sixteen feet wide, a quadriptych painted on four sections.

Jaune Quick-to-See Smith "sometimes incorporates glyphs or collage in the background of large iconic figures," observed Phoebe Farris in *Feminist Studies*, and "her narrative paintings always convey humor with a prominent political message that consistently addresses issues of respect for nature, animals, and humankind. Smith refuses to use art materials that pollute the environment, take excessive storage space, or are costly to ship. Her large painting, *Trade Canoe: Gifts for Trading Land with White People*, features Asian-made trinkets such a tomahawks, beaded belts, and feather headdresses hanging on a chain above the Flathead Salish canoe."[19]

Jaune Quick-to-See Smith has painted many variations of the trade canoe with natives and animals and abstract contours in natural motion. The canoe scenes reveal totemic associations, bird and animal representations, patterns and layers of color, rabbit and coyote, figures in flight, a bald eagle, horses, an owl, simulated totem poles. *The Trade Canoe: The Dark Side*, a triptych, shows George Armstrong Custer on one end of the huge canoe and a native on the other end, and the mountains are simulated in the middle of the canoe. The Trade Canoe Series contains more than twenty original paintings, including two canoe sculptures.

The cosmototemic scenes and portrayals by some native artists in Canada and the United States carry on the inspired perceptions of natural motion, transparency, abstract contours, and visionary transformation common in the distinct scenes, figures, and designs of ancient cave art and en plein air scenes on stones. Norval Morrisseau, for instance, painted radiant scenes of natural motion, contours of shamanic forms, transparent animals, and creature transmutations. The untutored artist was probably born at the Sand Point Reserve, or Bingwi Neyaashi Anishinaabek, near Lake Nipigon, Ontario. There he was inspired by the ancient rock art and later created similar cosmototemic images and shamanic portrayals.

Morrisseau was an artist for more than forty years. He first created images on birch bark and hides. Later he painted the plane dimensions of intricate designs, spirit lines, cubist contours, great totemic birds, and in the bold hues of nature. Morrisseau matured in the presence of the mighty shamans and healers of the *midewiwin*, or the Grand Medicine Society, the spiritual and totemic healers of wounded souls, and in the presence of the pastors and priests of Christianity. Jesus Christ was a native shaman in one of his inspired portrayals. God the Son and the shaman, a double incarnation, with his head raised and to the side, embraced a totemic crane and two other birds in the backlighted halo of the sun.

The Road Home was an exhibition of emotive scenes and recollections of a native residential school painted by Robert Houle. The moody colors were visceral memories, natural motion, and the gestures were elusive. David McIntosh observed in the exhibition catalogue that the palette was gaudy, and a "remarkable feature" of the art "is the sense of movement." The scenes, in other words, were the natural motion of shadows and memories.[20]

Carl Beam is an extraordinary visionary and innovative artist. The traces of elemental scenes of natural motion, contour overlays, and transparencies are present in his elusive creations of manifold images and chronicles. Beam is one of the most intricate cosmototemic artists of natural motion and the contradictions of continental liberty. The native scenes in his intricate miscellanies create a tricky narrative of resistance and survivance. He dismantles obvious images in the presence of others, Christopher Columbus on one panel and a common electric meter in another panel, and to double the creative irony an elk afloat with bloody handprints on the canvas.

Sitting Bull, in a rouge hue, stands alone in one panel, a posed photograph, and in the other panels a railroad engine and scenes of the dissection of whales. *Big Things*, in *Carl Beam: The Whale of Our Being*, and other scenes, are the taut and tired remains of representation in a tragic civilization. Samuel Beckett, shamans, animals, and movie actors in the natural motion of ancient scenes gather in the muted wash, blue, rouge, and newsprint.[21]

Neo-Glyph I, an emotive scene of a raven, buffalo, and a nude political prisoner, could have been painted in the wall of a cave. Rouge dots, the celestial decoration on ancient stone, and contours of natural motion portray the shamanic resurrection of a bare and desolate native Wichita woman who was decorated with costume jewelry. William Soule had photographed the woman and other political prisoners at Fort Sill, Oklahoma. Beam created a sense of survivance with one posed photograph, and the collage of memory is forever in motion, a natural resurrection of cave art.[22]

"Beam most enjoys creating pieces that challenge and engage the viewer," observed Allan Ryan, and "the power to make meaning from juxtaposing objects and images is at the heart of Beam's art, especially his installations. It derives more from traditional shamanic practices than from mainstream art making."[23]

Rick Bartow revered the original markmakers, and rightly avowed an aesthetic association with the ancient painters on granite, sandstone, birchbark, and wood and in the great shadows of primeval caverns. The visions and natural motion of painted bears, horses, birds, and other creatures in totemic scenes are in transmotion, or visionary motion. The ancient traces and abstract guises, fusions, and colors are relevant in the art of Mark Chagall, Chaïm Soutine, George Morrison, Fritz Scholder, Horst Janssen, Francis Bacon, and Rick Bartow.

Bartow creates marvelous scenes of visionary motion, and his art reveals the countenance of humans, animals, and birds in a great union of native consciousness, the scenes of a bygone tradition of totemic liberty. Natural motion is obvious in the migration of birds, murmuration of starlings, traces of the seasons in willow and sumac, and imaginary shadows, shamanic visions, and the totemic torment of transmutation in dreams. The totemic rights and images of motion are unmissable in the masks of bears, hawks, mongrels, and coyotes and mark an ethos of native creative art. Bartow continues these ancient practices of transmotion and totemic liberty.

David P. Becker observed in "The Visionary Art of Rick Bartow," the "first aspect of his revelatory art that strikes the viewer is its sheer visual intensity, the saturated resonance of color combined with the determined energy of markmaking."[24] *Things You Know but Cannot Explain*, the thematic exhibition of Bartow images and sculpture scheduled at several museums, is presented in five interrelated sections: "Gesture," "Self," "Dialogue," "Tradition," and "Transformation." The strange contortions of creatures, shadows, and erasures, are "Gesture," the imaginary motion and visions of a painter. Shadows were once a vital presence in native stories and art, and with no discrete source. "Self" is elusive, a shadow, "the way we reveal our-selves, we let our life shine," said Bartow. He created a sense of totemic transformations and presence. "Dialogue" is a relation with the artistic visions of other painters, the motion, tease, and contact faces of animals and birds.[25]

Danielle Knapp pointed out that "movement and physical gestures are sublimely expressed through a variety of ways" in the paintings of Bartow: "Limbs are twisted and extended beyond physical reality; beings appear to scream or sing via a contortion of features and a layering of faces. Bartow's men, women, birds, and beasts are so convincingly poised for action that they seem as though they could spring to life at any moment."[26]

The triptych PTSD, for instance, confronts a "dark reality and shows how his experiences in a war he did not understand or support continued to shape his identity several decades later," observed Becker.[27] Bartow painted three chalky masks, each outlined in blue, marked with red, and toothy gestures, fear, desire, and mouth were erased with black, and the masks became a dialogue of similar triptych faces by Francis Bacon.

The traditional scenes are in natural motion, and not an aca-demic sidetrack or closure of cultural representations. Artistic transformations are visionary, totemic raptures are sublime, and the contorted coyotes, bears, and avian predators are imagined with beaks and toothy masks. These are original totemic visions.

Bartow creates marvelous visionary characters in the faces of creatures, and his paintings reveal that memorable union of humans and animals, a totemic liberty. Three years ago Bar-tow granted me permission to use *Raven's Dream*, pastel on paper, for the cover art of my historical novel *Blue Ravens*, about Native American soldiers in the First World War.[28] The imaginary motion, a distorted face with a rough bloody wash, a yellow hand of malady, and a bold black raven outlined in blue, became a dialogue of visions between the painter and the author. Many readers were convinced at the time that the painting had been commissioned for the novel. I had imagined in words the stories of war and scenes of blue ravens in the late glance of sunlight, and the painter had envisioned a similar visionary scene of natural motion on paper, a union of art, motion, and totemic liberty.

The elusive traces of cosmototemic natural motion, or transmotion, are revealed in dreams, stories, paintings, memory, literary art, movies, and cultural survivance. Totemic motion is observed on stone and bark, ancient cavern art, native dream songs, the contemporary portrayals by native artists, and easily perceived in a singular cinéma vérité project of documentary movies created on the Navajo Nation.

John Adair, the cultural and visual anthropologist, and Sol Worth, the painter and photographer, conducted a film project almost fifty years ago at Pine Springs, Arizona, on the Navajo Nation. The project considered the distinct cultural perceptions of native participants, and with only a basic technical introduction to the use of cameras. The seven documentary movies, short and unedited scenes of native motion in ordinary cultural experiences, were created without the obvious experience of film editing or production.

Adair and Worth noted in the introduction to *Through Navajo Eyes* that the study is "how a group of people structure their view of the world—their reality—through film." The authors inquired, "What would happen if someone with a culture that makes and uses motion pictures taught people who had never made or used motion pictures to do so for the first time?"[29] That context of native reality was an invitation to natural motion, a discrete perception of cultural gestures and action over abstract descriptions or edited filmic scenes.

The philosophical queries about the structures of language and unique cultural perceptions of reality were derived from specific ideas and discussions of the linguistic relativity of native languages and based primarily on the learned observations of Wilhelm von Humboldt, Franz Boas, Edward Sapir, and Benjamin Lee Whorf. The general outcome of the comparative studies of the structures of language and worldviews became widely known as the Sapir-Whorf hypothesis; however, the impressive idea that language and thought structured reality has never been fully accepted as a linguistic principle or theory.

Von Humboldt observed that language is a diversity of worldviews, not only a diversity of sounds and signs. Franz Boas wrote that there is a direct relation between language and culture. Edward Sapir was more direct and declared the similarities of two languages do not represent the "same social reality." Yet he pointed out that some distinct "unrelated languages" do share the similarities of one culture. Benjamin Lee Whorf studied the languages of the Inuit, Hopi, and others and observed that nature was "dissected" in distinctive categories by native languages. The "picture of the universe," in other words, was not structured in the same way.

Adair observed that the "Navajo are a people for whom motion is central to language and to major areas of their cultural life."[30] Navajo is a language of action, mainly verbs, and that sense of natural motion is observed in the cultural practices of weaving, sand painting, dancing, and walking. The knowledge of these images and visions of natural motion were sustained in cinematography.

"Almost all the films made by the Navajos portray what to members of our culture seems to ban as an inordinate amount of walking." The movies portrayed scenes of ordinary motion, even mere feet in motion, and a shadow "walking across the field," noted Adair.[31] The selected lines "Feeling light within, I walk. . . . With beauty all around me, I walk" are translations from the ceremonial songs of the Yébîchai, or Night Chant. Walking is a natural cultural motion, and walking in a song is a poetic visionary motion.

Adair noted that the weaver in one movie "spends fifteen minutes walking to gather vegetables for the dye, walking to collect roots for soap, walking to shear the wool," a cul-

Cosmototemic Art

tural portrayal of natural motion. Only a few minutes of the twenty-two-minute movie focused on the actual weaving. In another untutored cinéma vérité movie, "the mask of the Yébîchai walks and walks searching for the turning wheel." The portrayal creates a sense of "animism" in a "natural environment."[32] The wheel moves behind a building, and the camera follows the natural perception of the hidden motion and was not edited to show only the actual presence of the wheel.

8

Native *Nouveau Roman*

Dead End Simulations of Tragic Victimry

T he chase notes of discovery were easier to overcome with irony than the gossip theories of native cultures, the persistent and reductive reviews of natives in literature as romantic fades of victimry. The native stories of survivance are an unmistakable contrast, the visionary narratives of resistance and natural motion that create a sense of presence over monotheism, historical absence, cultural nihility, and victimry.[1]

Father Aloysius Hermanutz, Benedictine priest at the White Earth Reservation, "was constrained by holy black and white, the monastic and melancholy scenes and stories of the saints" in my historical novel *Blue Ravens*. "Black was an absence, austere and tragic. The blues were totemic and a rush of presence. The solemn chase of black has no tease or sentiment." Black constrains natural motion and the "spirit of natives, the light and motion of shadows. Ravens are blue, the lush sheen of blues in a rainbow, and the transparent blues that shimmer on a spider web in the morning rain. Blues are ironic, and tease natural light. The night is blue not black."[2]

God, "If You exist, make me blue." Yes, "make me blue, fiery, lunar, hide me in the altar with the Torah! Do something, God, for our sake, for mine," declared Marc Chagall in *My*

Life, an early autobiography.[3] Blue Chagall was a metaphor of natural motion and apparently was not intended to represent sadness or desolation; rather, he meant to be dreamy, an artistic, visionary presence, "make me blue."

Chagall painted humans and other creatures blue, rabbis, fiddlers, and horses green, and some of the figures in his paintings were taller than houses, some standing on the roof of a house or soaring overhead, over his home village, Vitebsk, Russia, on the Pale of Settlement. These grand visionary scenes and creatures were represented and staged in a musical, then a popular movie by the same name, *Fiddler on the Roof*. The musical and motion picture depicted the dreams of the painter as commercial representations of religion and culture, a commercial product, in other words, and the transformation of a visionary image into a picture product that is easily recognized in popular culture. The Broadway musical production of *Fiddler on the Roof* was performed at least three thousand times more than forty years ago. The London production ran more than two thousand performances.

Today, anyone around the world could merely chant "tradition," with a particular musical lilt, and most people would recognize the musical and motion picture, clearly a commercial representation of a dreamy, visionary painting of a rabbi playing a fiddle on a house in Vitebsk. The motion picture is a commercial simulation, of course, but wrongly a representation of culture or religion.

Chagall was never a commercial painter. He was an original, visionary artist, not a realist, not an artist of cultural representations. Yet sometimes, as in the musical and the movie, his wonderful dreamy, mythical green rabbis became commercial products, but, on the other hand, his painterly scenes were more accessible and visible, and to a much larger audience.

George Morrison was Anishinaabe, an artist and citizen from the Grand Portage Reservation in Northern Minnesota, and he became a famous international abstract expressionist painter. But the museum curators almost sixty years ago would not accept his work in major "Indian" or Native American exhibitions because the curators reasoned that his creative scenes were not traditional.[4] The curatorial exclusions were primarily based on the gossip theories of authenticity in traditional native art. Today, native artists might be excluded from exhibitions for political reasons, the real and personal politics of art, but not excluded because of racism, blood quantum, composition, or painterly style. Abstract expressionism was not considered or accepted as a native art style or practice until about fifty years ago.

Morrison was a brilliant expressionist painter, and he was highly praised among the most distinguished abstract expressionist artists in New York City and Europe. The provincial, protective, and patronizing museum curators at the time favored "Indian" art that depicted traditional themes, abstract designs, or representational portrayals of culture that museum viewers would recognize immediately, but not the visionary or expressionistic art. Native art had become a commercial traditional product.

These expectations of traditional themes, particular styles of realism, abstract patterns and designs, and cultural representations were probably more forcefully presented by Dorothy Dunn. She was admired for her dedication as a teacher but not for her pedagogy or methods of teaching native artists. She founded the Studio School as part of the Santa Fe Indian School in Santa Fe, New Mexico, in 1932. Dunn advanced the notion that natives were actually innate artists. Traditional native artists, she proposed, should not be distracted by the ideas and practice of landscape perspective or by the abstract expressionism of modern art. So she generously encouraged students to do outline drawings and flat colors to represent their cultures and traditions, not knowing that many of those cultural scenes, sacred dances and ceremonies, should not be represented in art or by any other means.

Dorothy Dunn "did not offer technical lessons in perspectival drawing or color theory, preferring that the students' natural ability and remembrance of their cultural traditions form the basis for their work."[5] Americans warmly reviewed and accepted separatist notions that natives were innate traditional artists, and that impression lasted for more than a generation. Many people thought that native art was an insight into native cultural traditions, a marvelous kind of artistic primitivism, that appreciative viewers could see directly into the tradition of natives through flat outlines and colors.

The progressive native art styles from traditional flat patterns to abstract expressionism were understood by many scholars and curators. These new expressionistic paintings and modern sculpture by young native artists were favored in reviews, exhibited widely, and represented in galleries. Slowly, the old styles of painting were retired and treasured by nostalgic museum curators.

This advance, however, from the flat traditional style to visionary abstracts and expressionism has not been widely appreciated in modern native literature. The scholars and reviewers who learned to appreciate the original styles of expressionism and ironic native modern art did not seem to understand the same necessary innovation and visionary expressions in native narratives or literary art.

French innovative literary artists of the *nouveau roman* have inspired and influenced authors around the world, including many contemporary native novelists. Yet French publishers seem to be adverse to innovative *nouveau roman* native authors. French publishers commonly provided translations of commercial native fiction, novels that reveal a romantic and tragic victimry over survivance and devoted histories about warrior cultures. The French, and readers in many other countries, mostly read in translation more commercial native literature than visionary innovative *nouveau roman* native narratives. These commercial novels are about traditional cultural simulations or the tragic and romantic themes of victimry. Other popular themes in translation are the adventure and romantic stories about spiritual healers.

Modern native authors might look back to the great French innovative authors of the *nouveau roman*, such as Nathalie Sarraute, Alain Robbe-Grillet, Georges Perec, Michel Butor, Maurice Blanchot, Marguerite Duras, and many others, but French publishers hardly ever consider in translation the innovative narratives of native literary artists. The creation of natural motion in literary metaphors and the ironic and necessary deconstruction of tragic themes and denouement plot lines were significant in the development of innovative native literature.

Native American literature, for the first time in literary history, can be clearly reviewed, discussed, and compared in four narrative categories: translated native stories and dream songs, early conversion and resistance literature published by natives educated at mission schools, native literary art, and popular native commercial fiction. These four styles or species of literary production require the same critical scrutiny as any other creative literature. The categories are not essentialist or absolute, of course, and are used only for purposes of comparative discussions. Native commercial fiction finds a much wider audience because the theme and style of the narratives focus more on tragic victimry, that is, the popular notions of terminal traditions and vanishing cultures.

Native literary art is a singular aesthetic, innovative and visionary, and the novelists and storiers of a native *nouveau roman* more often create scenes of survivance with metaphors of natural motion, or the *tropisms* of visionary motion and experiences, and irony that would confront the tragic closer of cultures and engender a sense of native presence over historical absence. Natives are generally an absence in history and must bear the literary duty to overcome the tragic wisdom of absence. The new literary art of survivance revives native irony and creates a sense of visionary motion and historical presence. Native literary art creates *tropisms* of survivance.

Nathalie Sarraute declared in the foreword to *Tropisms* that literary tropisms are precise tropes and observations, or "inner movements," and "hide behind our gestures, beneath the words we speak, the feelings we manifest, are aware of experiencing, and able to define. They seemed, and still seem to me to constitute the secret source of our existence, in what might be called its nascent state," as in consciousness. Tropisms are clearly revealed in native stories, dream songs, and the literature of the natural motion and the seasons. The tropisms and metaphors of natural motion created by native literary artists are scenes of resistance and survivance and "sources of existence."[6]

Jason Weiss points out in *Writing at Risk*, an interview with Nathalie Sarraute, that she "describes tropisms as the 'interior movements that precede and prepare our words and actions, at the limits of our consciousness.'" Tropisms "happen in an instant, and apprehending them in the rush of human interactions demands painstaking attention."[7]

Sarraute, a Russian Jew who studied literature at the Sorbonne, published *Tropismes* in 1939 in French. The first translation in English was published in 1963. Clearly, the premise of *Tropisms* is present in the innovative narratives of many modern native literary artists, that is, the "interior movements that precede and prepare our words and actions," but the customary plots and story lines of tragic victimry are apparently more popular in translation than the tropisms, creative sense of motion, and consciousness of innovative and visionary native authors translated and published in France.

Leon Roudiez argues in *French Fiction Revisited* that "Sarraute's tropisms, as she explained in the *Listener* some years ago, are those instinctive movements" that, according to Sarraute, "glide quickly round the border of our consciousness, they compose the small, rapid and sometimes very complex dramas concealed beneath our actions, our gestures, the words we speak, our avowed and clear feelings."[8]

Ezra Pound, editor, critic, and imagistic poet, created this memorable haiku poem, or concise aesthetic tropism, at the Concorde Metro Station in Paris in 1913:

Apparition of these faces in a crowd;
Petals, on a wet, black bough.

The faces in the crowd are ghosts, apparitions, and the faces are tender petals on a bough, a "wet, black bough." The images are tropism, an insinuation of interior motion and consciousness.

These tropisms and metaphorical gestures are what Nathalie Sarraute wrote about: to touch the mind and consciousness of the reader with a visionary image, a metaphor that is not a plot line representation or closure but rather the image teases the reader to imagine the scenes and stories.

This dramatic change of consciousness has already happened in native expressionistic art, but the appreciation of innovative native literary art, the native *nouveau roman*, has not been fully appreciated by commercial publishers in the United States or France. Native narratives of resistance and survivance have been published for more than three hundred years. Native literary art as original, dynamic, and innovative has become more familiar in the past two decades with publications in native book series by the University of Nebraska Press, University of Oklahoma Press, University of Minnesota Press, and the University of New Mexico Press.

Publishers and readers seem to be more interested in native novels that are simulations of "authenticity" rather than visionary, creative, and innovative narratives. Many readers would rather read a novel that gives them some general cultural information, yet the sources of most native literature are simulations or gossip theories of native tragedy, about native suffering, about the complications of the loss of traditions and cultures. Many readers reach for tragic victimry over narratives of survivance, and these tragic stories are provided and translated commercially day after day around the world.

Nathalie Sarraute conceived of literary tropisms in the creative practices of the *nouveau roman*, but paradoxically, French publishers apparently are more interested in the translation of cultural representations of romantic victimry over native scenes of survivance and innovative narratives. Publishers around the world must acknowledge, publish, and translate innovative native literature to confront the gossip theories of cultural fades and victimry. French readers must consider the tropisms of survivance in native literature and compare the *nouveau roman* to innovative native literary art, not the commercial literature that panders to the popular themes of tragic cultural victimry.

Consider the *nouveau roman* and innovative native literary art in the context of classical tragedy and comedy. Aristotle described tragedy, in the context of the theater, of course, as an action that arouses strong feelings. That imitation of action is not victimry. The imitation of action is a choice of metaphors, a tropism that arouses strong feelings, a sense of consciousness and natural motion, so that the reader appreciates the imitation, again the imitation of action that creates the sense of a tragic event, not the actual tragic victimry. The simulations of native victimry are not imitations of action in the sense of the classical theory of tragedy but rather the false simulations that create the romantic sentiments of realism and tragic victimry.

Aristotle observed a critical distinction between tragedy and comedy in theater and generally in literature. Comedy is a communal experience, and there is humor and irony, so to appreciate native experience and literary art, a reader must consider the theories of classical comedy over tragedy. Natives in general, however, have been consigned to the gossip theories of ethnography and publishers to the tragic mode, stoical, isolated, and tragic victims in literary art. Native painters

Native *Nouveau Roman*

have created a sense of presence in modern art, but the crucial literary art of survivance has not been fully appreciated by publishers and readers. Comedy, in the classical sense, would reveal more clearly a communal presence, a sense of irony, humor, and survivance in literary art.

"The books have voices. I hear them in the library," writes the literary artist Diane Glancy in *Designs of the Night Sky*:

> I know the voices are from the books. Yet I know the old stories do not like books. Do not like the written words. Do not like libraries. The old stories carry all the voice of those who have told them. When a story is spoken, all those voices are in the voice of the narrator. But writing the words of a story kills the voices that gather in the sound of the storytelling. The story is singular then. Only one voice travels in the written words. One voice is not enough to tell a story. Yet I can hear a voice telling its story in the archives of the university library. I hear the books. Not with my ears, but in my imagination. Maybe the voices camp in the library because the written words hold them there. Maybe they are captives with no place else to go.[9]

The University of Nebraska Press published selections from *Designs of the Night Sky* and four other narratives by native literary artists in *Native Storiers* in 2009. The *Native Storiers: A Series of American Narratives* has published innovative, emergent novels and avant-garde narratives created by native literary artists. The authors of these original narratives created tropisms and styles that portray unusual and diverse characters, experiences, and points of view. The literary styles register, construct, or depict a perception and ethos of survivance.

"Columbus landed in the second grade for me, and my teacher made me swallow the names of the boats one by one until in the bathtub of my summer vacation I opened my mouth and they came back out—Niña, Pinta, Santa Maria," writes Stephen Graham Jones in *Bleed into Me*. The boats "bobbed on the surface of the water like toys. I clapped my hand over my mouth once, Indian style, then looked up, for my mother, so she could pull the plug, stop all this, but when I opened my mouth again it was just blood and blood and blood."[10]

Many native innovative narratives bear the traces and tropisms of oral storiers and, at the same time, initiate a new aesthetic convergence of literary art. Clearly there are many cultural distinctions, ambiguities, and exceptions, but the literary practices, pleasures, and original flight of native literary artists are more significant than the mere simulations of commercial romance and victimry.

Native narratives that easily reach a wide audience may portray the generic and romantic simulations of tragic victimry, that familiar sentiment in commercial native literature. Literary tragedy is a serious occidental practice, and a dubious imitation of action that may represent the demise of character or fortune in literature and popular culture.

Native storiers create action in scenes and character by natural reason, visionary motion, transformations of nature, and an active sense of presence and survivance. Some readers are more familiar with the cues of realism, character motivation more than visionary transformation, closure or denouement, and the simulations of tragic victimry.

The five narratives selected for publication in Native Storiers: A Series of American Narratives demonstrate a distinctive literary aesthetic. Early native storiers, the ancestors of modern writers, created a sense of presence by natural reason, sound, motion, traces of the seasons, by imagistic tropisms and totemic associations of birds and animals, by visions and transmutations, and by evasive, unrehearsed trickster stories. The ethos of presence and survivance, or spirited transmotion, tricky conversions of reality, and a visionary motion of continental liberty are the unmistakable cues and traces of a new aesthetic in native literary art.

"Forgetting. That's what this is really about: trying to sort out those times in your experience with someone that you'd just as soon not have to carry around with you for the rest of your life. They tell you it's about remembering, when they try to sell your family the inspiration cards with your entry and exit dates and some moving verse," wrote Eric Gansworth in *Mending Skins*. He continued,

> These suspension straps lower me into the hole then slide out from under me, and the last ritual begins. They want to pretend they're helping to bury me, my last mortal remains, but what they really drop down into this deep hole are memories, unwanted, muddy thickly clotted memories, laced with roots and worms and beetles, the occasional termite.
>
> My father is first, I recognize his hand immediately. He lets the dirt fall in hard clumps, hitting the top of my urn. I wonder if he's using two hands to pick up a large enough chunk. He's looking to make a dent, leave a mark, anything. . . .
>
> My mother is second and even a little unsteady in the way she tosses the dirt in. She sprinkles it like she would powdered sugar on top of fry bread on occasion. She doesn't want to give up that many memories, but I know the ones she's dusting me with. They are those last few weekends I come home on leave, saving all my pay so I can get back here, and she grows more and more busy every time I return. That last time she asks me not to come back, that it's too hard to see me leave, and I can see she'll be relieved when I head out for Vietnam for good, so she can begin the forgetting process in earnest. She's been rehearsing for this minute going on five years.[11]

Native ancestral storiers hunted for imagistic words and tropisms in memory, sound, shadow, chance, ecstatic conversions, the uncertainties of nature, and the natural motion of the seasons. Native literary artists create the tropes of oral stories in the silence of narratives and in the scenes of eternal motion, totemic transmutation, pronoun waves, gender conversions, the presence of other creatures, visionary voices, and with a sense of presence. The native *nouveau roman* aesthetic practices alight in the innovative stories and narratives of many literary artists.

"The ceremony is ended. The people are lining up for the giveaway. Oscar pushes you into line, and you move forward shuffling in the snow. The woman ahead of you says to her companion something about that red blanket on the end and she hopes it's still there when it's her turn. The line moves forward, pauses, moves forward, and the pile dwindles some and it's your turn, but you stand there and wonder what on earth you would do with any of this stuff. You could always use the groceries, but it feels silly to carry it back on the bus," writes Frances Washburn in *Elsie's Business*. "You step forward. You reach up your coat sleeve, pull off your gold watch, and place it carefully on top of a ten pound bag of sugar. Step away. For Elsie. . . . There are at least a hundred people, and the dance is slow. When it is done the drums give a final thump. The *wicasa wakan* gathers the corners of the blanket together bagging the money in the middle, walks through the snow and hands it to you. Your arms are frozen at your sides."[12]

Michael Dorris, the late novelist, argued against the aesthetic distinctions of native literature. He declared there was "no such thing as Native American Literature, though it may yet, someday, come into being."[13] He was wrong, of course, and other authors and critical interpreters of native literature have also resisted the concept of a singular native literary aesthetics.

David Treuer asserted in *Native American Fiction: A User's Manual* that the "vast majority of thought that has been poured onto Native American literature has puddled, for the most part, on how the texts are positioned in relation to history or culture." He noted, "We can evoke a connection to the past in our writing, but novels are wishes, fantasies, fairy tales."[14] That crude reduction of native visionary and ironic literature to "wishes, fantasies, and fairy tales" is a deceptive ploy of nostalgia and dominance. Treuer, a novelist, critiques only the practice, stature, and representations of native literature, but for some obscure reason he rarely observes in his commentaries the marvelous visionary traces of native transmotion and aesthetics.

Louis Owens observed in *Other Destinies*, "There is indeed such a thing as Native American literature," and "it is found most clearly in novels written by Native Americans." Despite "the fact that Indian authors write from very diverse tribal and cultural backgrounds, there is to a remarkable degree a shared consciousness and identifiable worldview reflected in novels by American Indian authors, a consciousness and worldview defined primarily by a quest for identity."[15]

The traces of native experiences, oral stories, totemic associations, and consciousness are easily reviewed in the sentiments, figuration, natural motion, metaphors, and syntax of distinct native narratives. The hucksters of a more secure position with commercial publishers strain to deliver the spurious notions that obscure the distinctive practices of a native literary aesthetic.

Consider, for instance, the native storiers who created animal characters with a tricky sense of consciousness, the natural motion of a native aesthetics of survivance. Many contemporary native novelists created the totem tease and consciousness of animals in dialogue and descriptive narratives and overturned the monotheistic separation of humans and animals. N. Scott Momaday, Leslie Marmon Silko, Gordon Henry, Diane Glancy, Stephen Graham Jones, Louis Owens, and other native authors have created memorable animals that reveal a native aesthetics in their stories and novels. Momaday created lusty bears, Silko native witchery, Henry and Owens spirited mongrels as distinctive characters in their novels. These practices and sentiments are a native literary aesthetics of totemic associations and survivance. "Stories with animals are older than history and better than philosophy," observed Paul Shepard in *The Others: How Animals Make Us Human*, but "history tries to describe the world as if it began with writing and only humans mattered."[16]

John Rogers, Momaday, Silko, Henry, Glancy, Owens, and many other native authors use metaphors as motion, as cosmototemic natural motion, and as comparisons, to be sure, but not as mere hackneyed similes, dead descriptions, or attributions about animal and human characteristics. Animals and humans are either compared, as in mundane similitudes, or, as in aesthetic native narratives, animals are characters, literary figures with voice, consciousness, and natural motion.

"I could read more in the swaying of the trees and the way they spread their branches and leaned to the wind than I could read in any books," wrote Wayquahgishig, or John Rogers, in *Red World and White: Memories of a Chippewa Boyhood*:

> I could learn much more from the smiling, rippling waters and from the moss and flowers than from anything the teachers could tell me about such matters [and] gain knowledge from my daily walks under the trees where the shadows mixed with the shifting sunlight and the wind fanned my cheek with its gentle caress or made me bend, as it did the trees, to its mighty blasts.
>
> I knew then, as I have since, that no amount of such learning that came to me in these schools would keep me from loving the things of Nature. . . . Always would the voice of the wind through pine needles or its rustling of the leaves in the sturdy oak and the towing maple bring to me a message that no book could give. Always would I long for the lakes and rivers and hills.[17]

John Searle, the philosopher of language, argued in his essay "Metaphors," the "knowledge that enables people to use and understand metaphorical utterances goes beyond their knowledge of the literal meaning of words and sentences." He wrote that a "literal simile" is a "literal statement of similarity" and that a "literal simile requires no extralinguistic knowledge for its comprehension." The "literal simile" is the most limited trope or figuration.[18]

Grey, the main character in *The Ancient Child* by N. Scott Momaday, "dreamed of sleeping with a bear. The bear drew her into his massive arms and licked her body and her hair. It hunched over her, curving its spine like a cat, until its huge body seemed to have absorbed her own. Its breath which bore a deep, guttural rhythm like language, touched her skin with low, persistent heat."[19]

Leslie Silko encircles the reader with a scene of mythic witches, an ironic metaphor of creation stories in *Ceremony*. The hardhearted witches actually invented white people in a competition, a distinctive figuration that overcame the mere comparison of natives with the extremes of racialism. Betonie, the old man, "shook his head. 'That is the trickery of the witchcraft,' he said. 'They want us to believe all evil resides with white people. Then we will look no further to see what is really happening. They want us to separate ourselves from white people, to be ignorant and helpless as we watch our own destruction. But white people are only tools that the witchery manipulates; and I tell you, we can deal with white people, with their machines and their beliefs. We can because we invented white people; it was Indian witchery that made white people in the first place.'"[20]

Louis Owens pointed out in *Other Destinies* that the words of Betonie and "the story of witchery underscore an element central to Native American oral tradition and worldview: responsibility." That sense of native duty and reliability reveals sentiments of survivance, a native aesthetics, and a metaphor that denies closure and victimry.[21]

Dorothy Lee declared in *Freedom and Culture* that the "Dakota were responsible for all things, because they were at one with all things." The sense of personal duty was also communal, but the sense of obligation to others revealed a distinctive cultural ethos: "The Dakota were responsible, but they were accountable to no one for their conduct." Responsibility was not related to accountability; "ideally, everyone was responsible for all members of the band, and eventually for all people, all things."[22] Native storiers and literary artists were responsible for the visionary presence of totemic animals and birds, and for the metaphors of natural motion over dead similes, but native storiers were not accountable for the fur trade.

Metaphor, observed George Lakoff and Mark Johnson in *Metaphors We Live By*, "is one of our most important tools for trying to comprehend partially what cannot be comprehended totally: our feelings, aesthetic experiences, moral practices, and spiritual awareness. These endeavors of the imagination are not devoid of rationality; since they use metaphor, they employ an imaginative rationality."[23]

Native literature has never been a newcomer in the course of resistance to dominance. Natives have resisted discovery and political tyranny for centuries, from the first stories of contact, the wily breach of trust in monotheistic empires, fascist cavalry soldiers, and the autocracy of federal agents, to the unbearable ironies of a constitutional democracy. The storiers of resistance were visionary, wise, ironic, and tricky.

Keeshkemun, for instance, the nineteenth century Anishinaabe storier and diplomat, teased a British military officer with the tropes of natural reason and survivance. The native envoy created a totemic sense of presence in a memorable riposte to military dominance: "I am a bird who rises from the earth, and flies far up, into the skies, out of human sight; but though not visible to the eye, my voice is heard from afar, and resounds over the earth."[24] The bird in mind was surely the totemic sandhill crane. Keeshkemun used an avian metaphor to evade the political dictates of empire conversions, and at the same time he sidestepped the obvious declaration that the Anishinaabe were loyal to the fur traders of New France.

N. Scott Momaday, Leslie Marmon Silko, Louis Owens, Diane Glancy, and many other novelists create animals and birds in dialogue and descriptive narratives with actual names, consciousness, metaphor, and allegory, a natural sense of presence that overturns the monotheistic separation of humans and animals. The similes that favor humans over animals, or animal similes that demean and deprecate humans, are common in commercial literature. Native visionary storiers and novelists create birds and animals with a sense of presence, not as separations from natural motion or totemic associations.

"The imperial ravens stole my lunch. I was sitting on a bench in the park when a palace raven soared from the crown of the Ministry of Justice building and, with a perfect, silent dive, snatched the last piece of my bento sushi," I wrote in *Hiroshima Bugi: Atomu 57*:

> Tokyo was firebombed at the end of the war and the ravens quickly moved to the secure trees of the Imperial Palace. The more guttural ravens of the industrial areas, nearby docks, and remote sections of the city, resent the imperial strain, their haughty relatives, the palace ravens who survived the war as aesthetic victims.
>
> The palace ravens search the restaurant trash at first light, and then, in smart teams, they raid the parks. By dusk they return to their roosts in the imperial sanctuary. My bento sushi became one of their stories of the day.
>
> I watched the ravens descend at great speed from nearby buildings, a trace of silent black motion, a perfect flight, and snatch a cracker from a child, a rice cake from a schoolgirl, a sandwich from a tourist, with impunity and no moral responsibility. These ravens are a tribute to a criminal empire, the great, tricky warriors of Hibiya Park.[25]

Natural motion is a heartbeat, ravens on the wing, the tease of plovers on the shoreline, songs of the season, the rise of whales, and thunderclouds. Transmotion is the visionary or creative perception of the seasons and the visual scenes and tropisms of motion in native art and literature. The literary sense of transmotion is an actual and visual image across, beyond, on the other side, or in another place, and with the native favor of presence.

The narratives in these five selections create a sense of native presence over historical absence, a visionary motion of survivance and liberty, not a commercial storyline, and never an unseemly romantic levy of separatism, retreat, expiration, or the dead end romantic simulations of heroic tragedy. These native stories and narratives clearly repudiate the gossip theory that native literature was a cryptic representation of cultural victimry.

Ethnographic and literary gossip theories pursue but never inspire stories or entrust creative narratives by native novelists. Theories never anticipate visionary or innovative narratives and never precede the clever, artistic variations of storiers. Native visionary narratives are literary art, and theories are translations or uncertain interpretations of that tensive union of memory, tropisms, traces of convergence, tradition, culture, and the tease of native irony. Obviously natives are not the only authors in the world who create scenes of natural motion in literature.

Paul Cuffe was twelve years old when he made his first ocean voyage in 1808. He related in *Narrative of the Life and Adventures of Paul Cuffe, a Pequot Indian: During Thirty Years as Sea, and in Traveling in Foreign Lands*, a concise memoir, that "we had much rough weather; so much so, that we were compelled to throw overboard fifty tons of iron" near the Grand Banks.[26] Paul Cuffe, his father, Wampanoag and Ashanti from West Africa and the "wealthiest man of color in the United States," was an abolitionist and the captain of the merchant ship.[27] Paul Cuffe, the adolescent son of the sea captain with the same name, matured on the natural motion of oceans and whalers with his father for three years, and later he sailed on merchant ships and risky whalers around the world for more than thirty years. The narratives of his adventures were printed in 1839, twelve years before the publication of *Moby-Dick* by Herman Melville in 1851. The singular memoir of a native whaler and the marvelous novel are not comparable, but the selected scenes from each narrative reveal a heartfelt sentiment of natural motion and survivance.

Cuffe writes that several hundred miles from the coast of Brazil "we commenced fishing for whale, but for a time had bad luck, owing to the drunken habits of our Captain. We sunk twelve whales before we caught one. Then we caught six in the course of two weeks. I harpooned all these, and assisted in taking and towing them along side the ship. After we got a whale along side, we hitch our blubber hooks into the head, after severing it from the body, then, with our windlass, draw it aboard, and dip the oil out, which sometimes amounts to more than fifty barrels." Once the "mass of flesh is stripped from the carcass," the remains become the "sport of sharks, who feed upon the little flesh which remains after it has gone through the hands of the whalemen."[28]

The evocative narrative of whalers, the particular array of whale oil and blubber, were similar to the precise features of whale tails noted in *Moby-Dick*. The descriptive scenes of whales, distinctive tails, the heave of ocean waves, and the "sport of sharks" are the tropes of natural motion.

Rightly so, the great portrayals of whales are in natural motion, the scenes of transmotion and "panoramas" of the universe. Likewise the notable diction of the narrator and his astute manner, gesture, and maneuvers of words created images of natural motion in science, ideologies, and history. Ishmael created a figurative sweep of humans and whales in *Moby-Dick* and revealed a distinct sense of natural motion in a narrative of irony and chance.

Herman Melville was thirteen years old when his father died in 1832. Seven years later the prospective teacher and engineer became a cabin boy on a merchant ship bound for Liverpool, England. Later, in 1841, he sailed on the *Acushnet* for the South Seas. The following year he was imprisoned as a mutineer in Tahiti. "In course of time, my thoughts became more and more prone to dwell upon foreign things; and in a thousand ways I sought to gratify my tastes," Melville wrote in *Redburn*. And "as years passed on, this continual dwelling upon foreign associations, bred in me a vague prophetic thought, that I was fated, one day or other, to be a great voyager."[29]

Ranald MacDonald was Chinook, a native sailor on the *Plymouth*, a whaler in the northern seas of Japan. He landed by feat and chance on the islands of Rishiri and Yagishire in 1848, about six years after Herman Melville sailed near Japan and three years before Ishmael, equally by feat and chance, survived on a coffin when the great white whale Moby Dick dashed and sank the *Pequod*.

The Ainu rescued MacDonald from his overturned boat. His exotic presence was reported to the occupation shogunate of Hokkaido. MacDonald, the first Native American Indian to "discover" Japan, was held in a special residence or prison for about ten months at the port of Nagasaki. He taught English to fourteen interpreters six years before Commodore Matthew Perry arrived to open the ports of Japan.

The Ainu greeted MacDonald when he came ashore in Hokkaido. They rubbed their hands together, stroked their beards, and made guttural sounds. The Ainu customs of tattooing were distasteful to the native Chinook from the Pacific Northwest of the United States. Herman Melville was even more troubled by tattoos. He observed a man on his back in pain and agony. "His tormentor bent over him, working away for all the world like a stone-cutter with mallet and chisel," he wrote in *Typee*. Already "his cheek had been pierced by the point of a spear, and the wound imparted a still more frightful expression to his hideously tattooed face, already deformed by the loss of an eye."[30]

Native *Nouveau Roman*

Melville never hesitated to point out other cultural practices: "Civilization does not engross all the virtues of humanity: she has not even her full share of them. They flourish in
greater abundance and attain greater strength among many
barbarous people. The hospitality of the wild Arab, the courage of the North American Indian, and the faithful friendship
of some of the Polynesian nations, far surpass any thing of a
similar kind among the polished communities of Europe."[31]

Ronin Browne, the *hafu* narrator of *Hiroshima Bugi*, wore
invisible tattoos on his chest and back. "Atomu One, Eight Fifteen," printed on his chest, is the time and date of the nuclear
destruction of Hiroshima. The tattoos on his back were floral,
pictorial. Atomu One became the new solar calendar that starts
with *hibakusha* pain, torment, and misery. The invisible tattoos
were marks of singularity. Atomu One tattooed on his chest was
a remembrance of the ghosts of *atomu* children, as invisible as
his tattoos, and to honor the *hibakusha* survivors of Hiroshima.[32]

Ronin is loyal to the *kami* spirits of thousands of children
who died when the atomic bomb destroyed Hiroshima. He
resisted, countered, and accosted those who endorsed notions
of fake peace, and he obstructed museums in the name of war
and peace.

"Death is my vision in the faint light of morning," he wrote
on a bakery napkin. Ronin mentioned an unnamed master,
who "said, 'We are separated from a sense of presence because
of our fear of death.' Consider the instance of nuclear wounds
every morning and the fear of death vanishes. The samurai
warrior is never shamed by the fear of death."[33]

Lafcadio Hearn, the Irish and Greek storier of Japan, and
Ronin Browne were both inspired by the story of Urashima
Taro. They were drawn to the sea, and to the vision of magical
flight. Ronin once dreamed he was a totemic sandhill crane
and soared out of sight. Taro, Ronin, and Hearn were roamers
transformed by the spirit of a crane feather in the story. They
are drawn to the sea and vanish in magical flight.

Literary theories may stimulate the discourse to compare and construe the apparent evolution of literature, but the traces and perception of natural motion, tricky turns of imagery, and the visionary reach of native narratives forever haunt the translators. Some readers consider literature a mere representation of culture, and others observe the bloodline or reservation pedigree of the author as a freaky source of authenticity. Some theorists, however, have gone astray in the shadows of literary art, seduced by their own romantic imputations or reversions, deceived by the steady simulation of cultural authenticity, and the ideologies of racialism advanced by the deniers of chance and survivance.

Literary historians and gossip theorists who endorse the essential representations of traditions to secure literature as liturgy ignore and at times inhibit the actual practices of literary art. The liturgical cruises into the native past only divert and misrepresent the creative visionary energy of traditions, as if the practices of literary art were structural, an architectural concept that defines only the linguistic and material connections, an imperious declaration of academic sovereignty over visionary native literature.

"I begin to think the books want me here. They want me to hear what they say. They talk from the written word," wrote Diane Glancy in *Designs of the Night Sky*. She wondered, "Maybe writing doesn't kill the voice. Put it in a grave. Maybe writing isn't the destroyer people think it is. . . . Sometimes I know the murmurings I hear are the voices struggling to cover themselves; to get out of the books. But where would they go?"[34]

9

Time Warp Provenance

Heye Obsessions and Custer Portrayals

Only a native novelist would envision a marvelous symposium on provenance at the Smithsonian National Museum of the American Indian, and with submissions from George Gustav Heye, the obsessive collector of native art and cultural objects; Leonard Baskin, printmaker and sculptor; and four native artists, David Bradley, Carl Beam, Daphne Odjig, and George Morrison. Heye, the tall stout collector in tight narrow shoes, and four distinctive artists are associated in a virtual presence to consideration native objects of art in galleries and museums and to mediate on the critical speculation that every collector has learned to cut and barter for the provenance of original native art and cultural objects.

Native provenance is visionary and ceremonial, more than the history of ownership and custody. The sources of the actual creation of traditional objects, medicine bundles and kachina figures, and the images and scenes of a native painting, representational, impressionist, abstract, cubist, expressionist, or collage, are the heart of native provenance. The second cue of provenance is the history of commissions, possessions, gossip theories, and recorded value of native art objects.

Native ceremonial objects and artistry are unmissable, but the testimony of provenance is elusive and complicated by the art collections of private and public museums. The provenance of many native objets d'art is traced to stories of a visionary presence, once a source of cultural identity, and to the protocol of galleries, the international commerce of art, and outright thievery. Native medicine bundles, masks, and every sacred object were sources of personal visions, cultural revelations, and stories of natural motion, and, at the same time, the evasive recounts of obsessive collectors.

George Gustav Heye, the obsessive collector, died more than sixty years ago, yet his name is a silent declaration of provenance associated with close to a million native art objects, kachina figures, medicine bundles, masks, baskets, blankets, pottery, hide robes, and clothing, and an incredible archive of more than a hundred thousand images in the permanent collection at the Smithsonian National Museum of the American Indian on the National Mall and at the George Gustav Heye Center in New York City.

Heye started his obsessive collection of artifacts at the turn of the twentieth century and established the Museum of the American Indian in Upper Manhattan in 1922. He died thirty-five years later. The museum was endowed but underfunded and was closed in 1994. That same year the Gustav Heye Center opened in the United States Custom House on Bowling Green in Manhattan. Most of the objects in the extensive collection were moved to the Smithsonian National Museum of the American Indian, and since then a significant number of sacred objects have been repatriated to native communities.

"Few Americans had ever heard of the Museum of the American Indian until a bitter fight surfaced recently over moving the collection, one of the finest of its kind in the world," out of the building in Upper Manhattan, reported William Grimes in the *New York Times Magazine* in 1988. Only the Smithsonian Institution and American Museum of Natural History in New York "rival the museum's holdings of Indian artifacts."[1]

"Heye was omnivorous and monomaniacal," declared Werner Muensterberger in *Collecting: An Unruly Passion*. To gather his collection, "once a year Heye purchased a new automobile and raced across the United States from coast to coast. Here and there he would stop, 'look up the local mortician and weekly-newspaper editor, and ask for word of people lately deceased, or soon likely to become so, whose possessions might include an Indian collection.' On these trips Heye also visited Indian reservations."

George Gustav Heye, a portly investment banker at the time, started his monumental collection in New York City. "'He would be fretful and hard to live with,' a former staff member remarked, 'until he'd bought every last dirty dishcloth and discarded shoe and shipped them back to New York. He felt that he couldn't conscientiously leave a reservation until the entire population was practically naked."[2]

Muensterberger observed that his "unrelenting obsession shows a solid measure of ambivalence toward the Indians. By stripping them 'practically naked' he carried home his badges of victory." Heye acquired his first native artifact, a deerskin shirt, and that started his obsession to collect native objects. "As the acquired object brings with it additional support and hence narcissistic enhancement, envy and brute sadistic instincts play a large part in the perpetual search for personal triumph in order to ward off one's susceptibility to helplessness and frustration." Heye was moved by a "hidden rage" and "obsessional control" of native cultural objects, declared Muensterberger.[3]

The political critiques and psychoanalytic observations of his monomania have never diminished the appreciation, value, and influence of his collection. The Smithsonian National Museum of the American Indian has apparently absolved the incredible obsessions of a private collector, yet the historical provenance of many native objects remains discreetly in the name of George Gustav Heye. His name as a collector, however, is forgotten with repatriation.

The actual provenance of the museum collection of native objets d'art is ironic, and the curators were right to resist the celebration of the obsessions and perversions of George Gustav Heye. The manners of possessive collectors of native cultural objects were unruly, and pushy, but the monumental collection of native cultural booty must always reveal the provenance and controversial accession practices of every collector, and especially the man whose fame was based only on his incredible cache of native art, George Gustav Heye.

Leonard Baskin, a printmaker and sculptor, celebrated native warriors in his series of lithographs, and with good reason despised George Armstrong Custer. All the same, he accepted a commission by the National Park Service to create several images in memory of the Battle of Little Bighorn. Baskin portrayed the tragedy with angular figures, the desolate images of the "last stand" of lonesome soldiers and the controversial portrayal of George Custer. An estimated one thousand native warriors had defeated five companies of the United States Seventh Cavalry near the Little Bighorn River in Montana on June 25, 1876. Robert Utley, a distinguished historian, wrote a concise account of the "last stand" for the commemorative guidebook published by the United States Government Printing Office.

Baskin depicted "Custer seated and in uniform," and "rendered him rather shaggy and with an apparently glazed look," observed Michael Kammen in *Visual Shock: A History of Art Controversies in American Culture*. Further, "Baskin also depicted the dead Custer naked, which is how the Indians had actually left his body." Later the artist commented in an interview, "Somehow one is glad. He would have made a terrible president."

Utley wrote in the National Park Service guidebook that the body of Custer "had been stripped but neither scalped nor mutilated." Custer partisans, enthusiasts, and the incredible Seventh Cavalry nationalists, however, bitterly protested the nude image created by Baskin. Utley declared later that he was "'appalled by the artwork" and would not permit his

Time Warp Provenance

name to be associated with the book" if it contained the nude portrait by Baskin. The historian complained that the nude image of Custer was "terribly disrespectful," and the artist was "impressionistic."[4]

Kammen pointed out that the "Park Service decided to resolve the issue by printing the guidebook with a limited number of Baskin's Indians and with a totally blank page. Any visitor who wanted to buy Baskin's dead Custer could do so and paste it" on the blank page. Custer "stripped" remained the same in the text by Utley. The irony is that the nude image was restored, with "no blank page" in the second edition of the guidebook. Kammen noted that later editions included more photographs and "historic artwork" and fewer images by Baskin: "The pictorial format of subsequent printings has more color illustrations added, but they are highly traditional and a sharp contrast with Baskin's stark depictions."[5]

Baskin "drew all of these kind of weird-shaped, impressionistic images of Custer and Indians," declared Utley in an interview with Ellen Foppes in *Pioneers of Public History*. He continued, "When I saw it, I just went into orbit. I said, You really have pulled a fast one on me here. . . . I'm a very good friend of the Custer family, and I know this whole thing is going to offend them, but what will really offend them is that one page that's got the dead, naked, and mutilated Custer."[6]

Wild West amateur historians and bridle path partisans of heroic, romantic portrayals of George Armstrong Custer persuaded the National Park Service to overlook historical revisionism. Baskin created an angular ironic image of the dead cavalry commander with a desolate gaze of glory gone astray, and that marvelous crease of native history has outlasted the park nationalists and insecure revisionists of the Battle of Little Bighorn.

David Bradley, the Anishinaabe painter and sculptor, created *Greasy Grass Premonition* with eight identical images of George Armstrong Custer in uniform, black hat, yellow scarf, gold epaulets, white gloves, with arms folded, and poised across the bottom of the canvas. The cartoon dream dots connect the truculent officer to a misty simulated ledger art bubble scene of native warriors and defeated soldiers of the Seventh Cavalry at the Battle of Little Bighorn in June 1876. The provenance of that scene cannot evade the unintended irony of conceit and defeat revised as heroic by the prairie partisans and revisionists of military history.

Carl Beam, an Anishinaabe artist from Manitoulin Island, Ontario, created painterly time warps of native provenance. The scenes of personal and political images and collage narratives are in visionary motion, the critical tours of cultural torment and backhanded historical notes about natives.

Beam entwined native figures, handprints, animals, numbers, poems, and narratives on a monumental linen canvas nine feet high and forty feet wide and teased every observer with the title of the painting, *Time Warp*. Twenty silhouettes of bears, a totemic parade, were painted across the top of the canvas, and four bears were hidden in a mist. Translucent figures, the ghostly outline of a horse with blue traces of bones, and handprints were similar to the ancient native images painted on the face of granite in the canoe country.

POEM FOR THE BASTARDS NUMBER 2 is the title painted in rusty red at the center of the huge canvas, above a narrative about a bear. "Interview with the bear went very well. I was surprised to find out that he was very fond of singing." The poem is the natural motion of a totemic time warp, a native dream song, and the sky loves to hear the painter and the bear sing.

Beam created translucent scenes with no horizons, and many images were obscured with a wash or paint spatters, but the painted narratives were readable. Sitting Bull, the Lakota spiritual leader, and many other images of native leaders were painted or pictured in collages. *Time Warp* was painted with "deep red and brown hues" and with "yellow, white and blue," observed Jane Horner in "Revolving Sequential: Concepts of Time in the Art of Carl Beam." The washes and thin or thicker paint "create shapes that appear alternately closer and father away, creating a palimpsest effect. Images shift from past to present and back again, drips evoke erasure and splatters add movement."[7] The scenes were spatial, images afloat, the painterly outlook of native survivance in the visionary motion of totemic animals and dream songs, and a sensory motion greater than structures of line and time.

Daphne Odjig, Potawatomi and Odawa, was born at Wikwemikong Reserve on Manitoulin Island, Ontario. She was an untutored artist of natural motion, and nurtured by her grandfather, a stone carver. "Life is a circle," she said many times, and "nature is full of circles."[8] Odjig created outlines and curved scenes with gentle hues of color in her early paintings, and that style became a signature practice of cubist contours with the bright tease of complimentary colors. The curves of every scene embraced the faces and figures that seemed to unfurl or meander in natural motion. These were visionary, expressionistic, and abstract scenes that prompted Norval Morrisseau to declare that Daphne Odjig was "Picasso's grandmother."

The Anishinaabe word *ojiig*, or *odjig*, means fisher, the totemic animal, similar to the marten. Daphne once used Fisher as a surname to avoid prejudicial comments about her native identity. Daphne moved to Toronto during the Second World War, visited museums, and was inspired by the great painters. Slowly she developed a singular style of outlines and curves, and her drawings and paintings were included in art exhibitions. The first solo exhibition of her paintings was at Lakehead Art Centre in Thunder Bay, 1967. She was forty-eight years old at the time, and the second exhibition was a year later in Brandon, Manitoba.

Daphne and other artists founded the Professional Native Indian Artists in 1973, or the Indian Group of Seven, including Norval Morrisseau, Alex Janvier, Carl Ray, Eddy Cobiness,

Jackson Beardy, and Joseph Sanchez. The group stimulated more attention and appreciation of creative native artists in Canada.[9]

Daphne received a commission from the Canadian Museum of Civilization and painted *The Indian in Transition* in 1978, a great visionary mural of native touch, relations, and encounters over three centuries. The mural, about eight feet high and twenty-seven feet wide, is painted with rusty reds, moody blues, and with traces of yellow, tawny, gold, and white streamers. The ovate eyes of natives were sincere, and with easy smiles, but other outline faces were tormented, empty white eyes, and one blue face of death, a communal response to the moment of deceptive discovery and colonial betrayal. The spectacular scenes were circular, faces afloat in natural motion on the canvas, and every figure was embraced and interrelated with the wave of others. The provenance of *The Indian in Transition* was more than three centuries down to that museum commission to create a visionary scene of natural motion and survivance by Daphne Odjig. "Lee-Ann Martin, curator of contemporary Canadian Aboriginal art at the Canadian Museum of Civilization," described *The Indian in Transition* as a "historical odyssey that begins before the arrival of Europeans, continues through the devastation and destruction of Aboriginal cultures, and ends on an expression of rejuvenation and hope."[10]

Janet Berlo and Ruth Phillips pointed out in *Native North American Art*, "Native artists in the United States and Canada used the more open definitions of Native art to move in a number of different directions." George Morrison, Truman Lowe, Emmi Whitehorse, Robert Houle, David Bradley and many other native artists "pursued the possibilities for the exploration of other kinds of aesthetic and iconographic problems."

Emmi Whitehorse, for instance, "credits her grandmother, a weaver, with having the most influence on her as an artist," observed Berlo and Phillips. Whitehorse said she aligned the process of her art with that of her grandmother. I start without an idea of what to paint, she said, and "my grandmother worked in that same fashion. She had nothing to go by when she worked at her loom. The bottom part would have a pattern, but the top part would just be all open space, so everything had had to be figured out immediately as she worked. That's the same way that I work."[11]

The provenance of paintings by Emmi Whitehorse should include the inspiration of her grandmother. The provenance of irony, however, was more elusive in native art. David Bradley, for instance, creates actual disguised figures in some of his acrylic narrative paintings. He transforms ordinary scenes with ironic images. One of his celebrated paintings, *How the West Was Lost*, shows three men seated at a game of poker. The cowboy carries a card tucked in his belt. The native with a bird perched on his shoulder bets an ironic estate, a "Deed to Indian Land." The Mexican sits under a crucifix. The three poker players are associated with the liquor bottles at their sides, Tequila, Fire Water, and Corn Whiskey. The provenance and influences of art that convey and portray political and cultural images may be obscure, intractable ironies, but never that difficult to substantiate.

David Penny observes in *North American Indian Art* that "some artists of Native Ancestry draw attention to the ironies inherent" in the images of Indians. Penny writes, "David Bradley's *American Indian Gothic: Ghost Dancers* appropriates Grant Wood's ironic painting of American cultural identity." The ironic traces were more memorable to natives than an "earnest prairie farmer with a pitchfork."[12]

David Bradley "often uses cultural icons in a style simultaneously vibrant and whimsical, playful and wry," reported *Indian Country Today*. "Bradley acknowledges the influence of many artists, including Diego Rivera, Fernando Botero, Henri Rousseau, Robert Rauschenberg," and "regionalists Grant Wood and Thomas Hart Benton."

Bradley declared, "By definition, by birth, Indians are political beings. That's our condition, our lot in life." My "narrative style," he explained, "allows me to tell complex stories, sometimes with complex iconography." Bradley is Anishinaabe, a citizen of the White Earth Reservation in Minnesota.[13]

Some museums and curators once impeded the exhibition of abstract expressionism, narrative, and ironic art by native painters because the content was not appreciated as clearly authentic or because the trace of traditional native sources was obscure. The cultural politics of separatist curators controvert the provenance of native art, creative expressions, and liberty.

George Morrison was a great abstract expressionist, inspired by traces of natural light, the shimmer of horizons over water, and the wave of surreal and expressionist painters in the 1950s of New York City. His abstract paintings have stimulated more expansive and resourceful interpretations of native provenance.

Morrison was Anishinaabe, a citizen of the Grand Portage Reservation in Minnesota. That cultural place and provenance, however, does not reveal the visionary sources of his aesthetic perceptions and original practices as an artist. Curators once refused to include his paintings in native exhibitions because abstract expressionism was not considered as an acceptable native provenance.

"The basis of all art is nature," he told Margot Fortunato Galt in *Turning the Feather Around*. The North Shore of Lake Superior "was subconsciously in my psyche, prompting some of my images."[14] Morrison was nurtured in the presence of indigenous sounds and light created by the seasons of the lake. He conceived of these natural images in the abstract rush of colors and memory, not in the traditional, academic, or popular representations of native cultures.

"My art is my religion," declared Morrison in *This Song Remembers*: "I've tried to unravel the fabric of my life and how it relates to my work. Certain Indian values are inherent—an inner connection with the people and all living things, a sense of being in tune with natural phenomena, a consciousness of sea and sky, space and light, the enigma of the horizon, the color of the wind."[15]

Morrison encountered Jackson Pollock, Willem de Kooning, Franz Kline, and other abstract expressionist painters at the Cedar Street Tavern in Greenwich Village. The "Cedar became a kind of intersection between the first and second generation of abstract expressionists" after the tragic death of Jackson Pollock. Morrison was an inspired expressionist painter, but he was never consumed by chauvinism, desperation, or a destructive artistic frenzy.

George Morrison died at age eighty on April 17, 2000, in Grand Marais, Minnesota. Mary Abbe reported in the *Minneapolis Star Tribune* that Morrison was "one of Minnesota's most distinguished and beloved artists." She noted that like "Claude Monet's famous Impressionist paintings of the Seine River, Morrison's abstractions reflected" Lake Superior's "everchanging moods. Their common motif is a horizon that burns fiery red, flares pink and modulates to dusky blues and dappled greens depending on the season, weather and time of day."[16]

10

Trickster Hermeneutics

Naanabozho Curiosa and Mongrel Chauffeurs

Naanabozho, that wily and elusive native trickster, created the earth with a few birds and totemic animals. The trickster creation stories were never the same, not liturgy or ceremony, and for that reason there were no singular epochs, evolution of bygone themes, or modern signatures. The most memorable literary imitations of trickster stories were visionary, not scrutinized or structural.

The Anishinaabe trickster teased stones, as his brother was a stone, and forever teased the crane, bear, loon, marten, and other totems of native ancestors. The trickster was a trope of natural motion and transience and derided gossip theory, churchy poses, and the monotheistic separation of animals and humans in the marvelous stories of totemic associations and visionary conversions.

Naanabozho, the first native trickster, told his brother the stone about his daily adventures. The trickster was the eternal tease of natural motion, and his brother was a standstill stone. The trickster and his stories grew larger, and the distances he traveled were longer by the story.

The trickster complained that he had to return to the campfire at the end of the day, so his brother the stone proposed a resolution, "Heat me in the fire, and then pour cold water over me." Naanabozho did just that with heat and water, and his brother the stone burst into millions of pieces that covered the earth. The trickster forever had a trace of his brother nearby to hear the stories, and now these new stories have readers.

The trickster stones were native estates and the natural motion of visionary stories but never a theocratic simulation of creation. The tease of trickster stories was inescapable and necessary in a world of terminal notions, separatism, the aftermath of monotheistic revisions of totemic associations with animals, birds, and trees, and the play of survivance over victimry.

René Girard observes in *The Scapegoat* that the trickster is "one of the two great theologies to evolve as a result of the sacrilization of the scapegoat." The two theologies, *divine caprice* and *divine anger*, provide "solutions to the problem that faces religious belief when the victim," and in this instance the simulation of the Indian, is the scapegoat of cultural dominance and ironically "becomes the means of reconciliation."[1]

The trickster stories of creation and totemic associations could be considered *divine caprice*, or the tease of one coterie of theology. Conceivably the outcome of separatism and the crass simulation of others, natives and primitives, could be perceived as the reconciliation of *divine anger*, or the clerical rage of monotheism. Trickster stories were never godly or ministerial, but the great tease of manners, convictions, and actualities delayed and deconstructed the churchy culture of scapegoats. The trickster tropes were more communal and comic than tragic separatism in language games. Trickster stories were wild and visionary, the tease of ethnographic manners that defied gossip theory and literal translations, and do not represent a cultural reality.

The trickster is a comic *holotrope*, or the visionary figure in constant natural motion, and the entire sense of presence in a comic scene with no burden of time or liturgy. Native storiers create trickster scenes with metaphors of motion and visionary totemic associations with animals, birds, and other crea-

Trickster Hermeneutics

tures. Consider the trickster stories as narrative chance and in this sense as comic and more communal than the crude folkloric structures of tragic victimry. "Imagination is not mere fancy," observed George Lakoff in *Women, Fire, and Dangerous Things*, "for it is imagination, especially metaphor and metonymy, that transforms the general schemas defined by our animal experience into forms of reason."[2]

The trickster was not a real person or "being" in the ontological sense. Tricksters were created in the stories of a language game and envisioned by visionary motion, tease, contradiction, and divine caprice The trickster is a *holotrope* and androgynous and resists gender translation and representation. The default pronoun of dominance was a conversion of the visionary presence of tricksters in stories, and a constant striptease was necessary in modern stories to undress the portrayal of existence and a native way of life.

The trickster was lascivious, an erotic shimmer in stories that liberated the mind and healed by chance, denial, and irony. The storier created a trickster that mediated wild bodies and terminal beliefs, a chance narrative that turned aside the litanies of monotheism.

Warwick Wadlington argued in *The Confidence Game in American Literature* that the trickster straddles oppositions and "embodies two antithetical, nonrational experiences of man with the natural world, his society, and his own psyche. On "the one hand," he explains, there is "a force of treacherous disorder that outrages and disrupts, and on the other hand, an unanticipated, usually unintentional benevolence in which trickery is at the expense of inimical forces and for the benefit of mankind."[3]

The tricksters in my stories turn federal agents into mannequins, monsters, and mooks, outplay reservation politicians at their own casinos, and persist in the academic creases of irony and visionary stories of survivance. Some trickster stories carry on steady teases of candor, cultural sincerity, and manifest manners. The best trickster stories always mock the old toadies gossip theory and victimry.

Naanabozho was a narrative chance, a cocky *holotrope* in a language game that teased the distinctions of voice, gender, causation, and human and animal representations. For instance, consider the trickster stories of the first dog driving school on the White Earth Reservation in Minnesota.

Reservation mongrels were at the very edge of a great leap in evolution. Stephen Jay Gould might have named this apparent breakthrough a canine "punctuated equilibrium" because many common mongrels were learning to drive at a native reservation school. Priests, nuns, and federal agents employed the certified mongrels as loyal chauffeurs.

There are three situations that brought about this discovery that ordinary reservation mongrels could drive and become chauffeurs. The tease of truth, of course, is in the practice of trickster stories.

First, everyone has observed the dogs that move into the driver's seat of parked cars at supermarkets. The dogs pretend they can drive. The tricky gestures are easily recognized, as most of the dogs never turn to look you straight in the eye. The mongrels avoid direct eye contact because a passerby might notice that the driver has the face of a dog. The serious mongrel drivers provide only a slight glance of the eye, not a full hairy face. Second, mongrels have been stealing cars on the reservations for many years. Who else would rescue cars from the parking lots at casinos?

The third reason is even more convincing. Mongrels and even pedigreed dogs, but not designer sleeve creatures with screechy barks, drove trucks during the Second World War. Amelia White, the eccentric daughter of Horace White, once editor of the *Chicago Tribune*, owned valuable property in the old Armenta Spanish Land Grant in Santa Fe, New Mexico. Amelia became a prominent breeder of Afghan hounds and Irish wolfhounds. The showy dogs were trained as warriors, truck drivers, chauffeurs, and served in Dogs for Defense. Many of these canine drivers were buried with military honors at the School of American Research in Santa Fe.

Almost Browne, who was almost born on the White Earth Reservation and made his first appearance in the stories of *Hotline Healers*, was convinced that the Dogs for Defense overcame the boundary of their pedigree, bested their ancestors in war, and were loyal chauffeurs. So he started the first documented mongrel driving school on a reservation in Minnesota.

The Animosh Driving School was established to provide mongrel chauffeurs for native elders to visit their relatives and friends. The word *animosh* means "dog" in the language of the Anishinaabe. The mongrels were never any trouble, and everyone knew that was the truth from trickster creation stories. Actually, the mongrel drivers were much more reliable than humans, partly because they never drank and drove at the same time.

The mongrel chauffeurs wore spiffy uniforms, bow ties, and white collars, and some natives said they looked just like the priests on the reservation. The first graduates of the Animosh Driving School were featured in many newspaper stories, and the Catholic Church hired the entire class of graduate mongrel chauffeurs.

The demand for mongrel chauffeurs increased every month. Children everywhere wanted dogs as school bus drivers. Success always creates problems, even for mongrel drivers on the reservation. Soon animal rights activists protested that dogs were being exploited as menial laborers and that it was cruel to expose dogs to the stress of traffic and air pollution. And what about union representation, the rights of drivers, fair wages, medical benefits, and retirement programs for mongrel chauffeurs?

The Animosh Driving School graduated and placed hundreds of certified mongrel chauffeurs over the years, including many school bus drivers. The animal rights activists continued their protest and initiated a state law to terminate mongrel drivers. No one on the reservation was really worried until a union of mongrel chauffeurs and bus drivers staged a protest and blocked traffic around the state capitols in Minnesota and California. At first the blockade was seen as divine caprice because children and pet lovers everywhere cheered their best friends behind the wheel, but then, when a mongrel cocker spaniel ran a school bus into a police car, the insurance companies pointed to a clause in their policy coverage: "no dogs allowed behind the wheel of a moving automobile." That single accident convinced the legislators of two states to vote against mongrel drivers.

The Animosh Driving School was closed that summer, but obviously the mongrel drivers would not turn their backs on the theory of "punctuated equilibrium." So they read the fine print of the first mongrel driving laws and decided to become mongrel aviators. The new state laws did not specifically deny mongrel aviation, and before long Almost Browne started the Animosh Microlight Aviation School on the White Earth Reservation.

Native trickster storiers were easily turned from the tease of mongrel chauffeurs and devout believers in baptism and salvation to wily shamans at the early woodland missions long before the revolution, centuries before the democracy, and separatist reservations. The veracious monks arrived by rickety canoes late in the fifteenth century and established Des Fleurs sur Gichiziibi Monastère, the Flowers of the Great River Monastery, to serve the Holy Rule of Saint Benedict at the headwaters of the native *gichi ziibi*, the "great river," or the Mississippi River. The French and Anishinaabe name preference for monastery over the Italian, I Fiori di Grande Monastero del Fiume, was never fully explained in the curiosa manuscript.

The monks encountered by chance, visions, and ironies of devotion the mighty tease of native shamans. The monks were solitary and susceptible to the tease of totemic animals, and one pious monk created erotic stories about lusty unions with animals at the headwaters, an entirely new totemic turn of associations. The inscrutable headwaters shaman and the monks created a racy manuscript of authentic animal curiosa stories.

The *Naanabozho Curiosa* was a monastic manuscript of curious sensual pleasures with animals first discovered by the respected antiquarian book collector Pellegrine Treves at an auction in London. Many historians considered the manuscript to be blasphemous, of course, and others were more cautious, and no one was convinced that a native shaman could overturn the vows of silent monks. There was no direct evidence that monks were ever at the headwaters. Indeed, the very notion of an erotic conversion with animals was heretical at any time.

Treves, an honorable man who was much admired by other rare book collectors, was convinced that the curiosa manuscript was authentic, although he never declared a position on sex with animals. Scientific and historical studies of the parchment and distinctive stylistics and patterns of the calligraphy revealed that the manuscript could have been created in the fifteenth century. The curiosa parchment was made with skins common to the totemic animals near the headwaters.

Professor Hagal Williamson, a conservative scholar of literature who underestimated early native populations and once scorned oral stories and histories, curiously turned to trickster stories and especially the curiosa late in his career. He reasoned in several critical essays that the "ecstatic tease of the stories was not inconsistent with the inspirational flourish of certain other early monastic manuscripts."

Slight hesitation, in this instance, became a virtue, as the crotchety old scholar announced several years later, and much to the surprise of his colleagues, that an archaeological report on a recent excavation revealed clear evidence of a monastery and monastic remains at Bad Medicine Lake, on what is now known as the White Earth Reservation.

The Black Death and the tyrannies of government had driven the monks to sea with their venerable manuscripts and a sublime vision of silence. The monks sailed west on the obvious course of the sun, over the ocean to the great rivers and lakes, and landed at the headwaters late in the summer two decades before the controversial adventures of Christopher Columbus.

Des Fleurs sur Gichiziibi Monastère was reputable in oral histories because of the extremes of devotion and the native heart dance of the old shaman woman. These strange men of unnatural silence were easily teased for their last flutters of erotic aversions. The sensual circumstances were even more crucial at the headwaters. Just as natural as the flow of cold water over the stones, the stony shaman, an old native woman, raised the ancient river mire with a beaver stick and taunted the crows and monks. She created a heart dance to mock the silence and pious service of the monks, and then she seduced them with erotic animal stories.

Monte Cassino, the celebrated sixth century monastery established by Saint Benedict in Italy, became the name of the new fifteenth century schismatic monastery at nearby Bad Medicine Lake. "Jesus Christ and the creatures of his creation never heard of the monks who would restrain their tongues in his name," the monks wrote in the curiosa manuscripts; "his creations are the sacraments of animism, and our eternal cause is to consecrate the beaver, the bear, and other divine and erotic totemic creatures."

The Monte Cassino on Bad Medicine Lake soon became the native center of the autumn heart dances and replaced the headwaters Des Fleurs sur Gichiziibi Monastère. Several hundred dancers, many from distant tribes, and thousands of animals came together at the monastery to tease each other, masturbate with polished stones and animals, carouse in the cold water, embrace erotic stories, and consummate their creation.

Trickster Hermeneutics

The *Naanabozho Curiosa* contains many actual stories of the sexual conversion of silent monks with the animals. The dedicated monks at the monastic masturbatory transcribed the descriptive and erotic curiosa entries in the manuscript. The calligraphic styles and signatures indicated that the curiosa stories were written over several generations; as one style would end, another style of calligraphy would appear in the precious manuscripts.

The sultry opossum, the least sociable of the arboreal marsupials, was one of the most erotic mammals at the monastery. The opossums were the first mammals "traded for spotted fawns and other sensual creatures at the autumn heart dances." The elusive opossum turns to the side and "raises the whiskers on her narrow snout at the touch of excitement." Several monks were aroused by the slow manner of these stout mammals with short legs, clawless big toes, and "the most erotic naked prehensile tails." The opossum have no hair on their ears either, a feature the monks raved about in the carnal trade stories of the heart dance.

The monks and the bears were natural masturbators. The shamans said the bear taught man how to masturbate when the two once spoke the same language. The smaller mammals at the heart dance bounced, shivered, and wriggled with sensual excitement, but the aroused bears roared and pounded the earth with huge paws.

"The most erotic features of the river otter are their webbed toes, and the sensual way they lope to the heart dance," was translated from the *Naanabozho Curiosa*. One monk wrote that he could not contain his lust and animal jealousy. He masturbated at least once, sometimes twice a day, and he was bothered that the other monks had "unclean thoughts of pleasure with his favorite river otter." The monk carried his erotic stone in a leather pouch close to his penis. The stone was used to arouse him as a memory of the otter.

The abbot of the monastery mocked the extremes of the

heart dance, the other monks loped like otter and beaver around the fire, and several monks wore simulated webbed toes. The monks revealed in the curiosa that they were overcome with the erotic totemic unions. One monk "lost his silent humor and heard no other creation but a river otter."

Native tricksters were present as ironic storiers in my novel, *Treaty Shirts*. The stories were related by seven native exiles from the White Earth Reservation with distinctive native nicknames, Archive, Moby Dick, Savage Love, Gichi Noodin, Hole in the Storm, Waasese, and Justice Molly Crèche. The exiles lived together on a houseboat named the *Baron of Patronia*, docked at Fort Saint Charles, an island near the international border of Lake of the Woods.[4]

Hearsay theories, or the theories derived from other abstract ethnographic models, beget a new ironic *naytive* literary theory, wrote Waasese, a nickname that means "a flash of lightning" in Anishinaabe. Yes, the necessary prefix "nay" to the theories of native literature that obscured a sense of natural motion and ironic stories. *Naytive* was a denial, a reference to the mushy naysayers of hearsay theories that restricted the interpretation of native literature to mere cultural themes and victimry.

The second discovery of natives was on the World Wide Web with computers, cellphones, and social media similes and created no sense of irony and no consciousness to perceive natural motion in native literature. The cut and cruises on the World Wide Web and the intentions of social media were irrelevant, not creative, and the pale blink of messages was only the slightest chance of literary metaphors, textual teases, or traces of irony that were at best unintended and lost in new electronic gossip theories.

Almost Browne, a native philosopher who was almost born on the White Earth Reservation, worried about the end of visionary native stories and taught others how to create new laser *holoscene* images and retrieve in natural motion the obscure metaphors, irony, and teases in native trickster stories. The laser *holoscenes* were figural and based on traces of a historical presence, however elusive or enhanced, and were original ironic portrayals in the night sky. The artistic abstractions were in the laser projection and motion, not in the fractured beams or shimmers of light. The laser images were always in motion and slowly dissolved in the manner of trickster stories, but not in the classical literary theory of denouement.

Gichi Noodin, or the "great wind" in Anishinaabe, related that Panic Radio has broadcast without a license at least three hours every night for more than forty years. The first broadcasts were from a rusty blue van parked near colleges and universities and from cardboard shadow cities under the interstate bridges in the city. The live broadcasts have continued on the international border in a houseboat named the *Baron of Patronia*.

The Baron of Patronia shouted his stories and waved at bears and missionaries but never delayed a confession or changed the weather or literature until he created the first panic holes and roared into the stony earth. The actual location of that maiden shout was a blue meadow near Bad Medicine Lake.

Natives were healed over the panic holes, and there were no dues or duties to the wily shamans or recitations to the priestly hustle and bustle of faraway salvation. Churchy enterprise healers conspired to shame and shut down the panic holes, but the shouters gathered in great crowds at country meadows, in city parks, and on riverbanks. They bellowed the very names, fears, politicians, federal agent betrayals, and the expensive venture cures of doctors over personal and communal panic holes of recovery.

The Baron of Patronia encouraged every panic shouter of survivance in the ruins of civilization and saluted once or twice a week on Panic Radio the native woman who roared over cardboard boxes with great musical vitality. The range of steady roars and shouts became regular recitals in the shadows of apartment towers, under interstate bridges, an overnight panic shout and remedy of city misery.

Captain Shammer, another character in trickster stories, was raised with three sisters, two brothers, and seven mongrels on the *Red Lust*, a houseboat on Lake Itasca. He inherited the captaincy from his father Eighty, a nickname related to the atomic number of mercury. The Shammer shouts were into the summer waves, and he was the first native since the fur trade to practice panic hole shouts in natural motion on water.

Shammer was later named chairman of native studies at the university, and straightaway he converted the faculty office hideouts to necessary courses of native studies, such as the program to train mongrels to detect the absence of irony, postindian holograms, a casino and slot machines in the library, Denivance Press, and the Panic Hole Chancery.

Justice Molly Crèche, a former native justice, related that autumn on the *Baron of Patronia* that the gaze of animals continued in stray trickster stories, and the stares of bears, wolves, or lynx were seldom averted with the disguise of hunters. The doctrines of the other, the gawky hunter in camouflage, the ruse of sounds, scents, and blinds, never lasted as a tricky evasion or escape from the steady gaze of animals. The gaze of the other was always there; to turn that gaze around, humans remained forever in the eyes of the other, in the magical eyes of bobcats, the steady stare of coywolves, and always in the compound eyes of blowflies. The gaze was bright and at night a glint, even in a trance, meditation, or a nightmare.

The court names and calendars of evolution created the disguises of the other, the animal other in monotheism, and natives were once wrongly considered the other creatures in the course of enlightenment and husbandry. The corrupted animals of civilization wore weighty clothes, giant wigs, top hats, spats, whalebone hoopskirts, and heavy powders to escape the steady gaze of totemic animals in the fur trade. The colonial men coveted the picture postcards of naked native women and carried out romantic fantasies on the hour. Many natives mocked the poses and evasions of the animal gaze with top hats, epaulets, and morning coats.

The gaze continues to uncover cultural disguises, and at the same time natives created a vital presence of the natural gaze in totemic unions, and without the evangelical shame of nudity. There were many other native gazes, the shamanic gaze, the ironic gaze, the gaze of adventures and survivance. The liberty gaze, erotic gaze, hunter gaze, godly gaze, medical gaze, hunger gaze, pity gaze, and a predatory gaze were once the prominent disguises of federal agents, and natives were once captured in the popular literary gaze of victimry. Native trickster stories reversed with mockery the ethnographic gaze of gossip theory.

11

Continental Liberty

The Spirit of Chief Joseph and Dane White

T homas Paine, the literary revolutionary, wrote in *Common Sense*, "It was the cause of America that made me an author" and "the cause of America is in a great measure the cause of all mankind." America "hath a blank sheet to write upon," he declared, but that notion of an empty space was the cause of colonial empires and the decimation of thousands of native families and cultures.

"Paine saw all of history turning on the outcome of the American colonies' conflict with Britain," observed Harvey Kaye in *Thomas Paine and the Promise of America*. Paine wrote, "The independence of America would have added but little to her own happiness, and been of no benefit to the world if her government had been formed on the *corrupt models of the old world*. It was the opportunity of *beginning the world anew*" and "of bringing forward a *new system* of government in which the rights of *all* men should be preserved that gave *value* to independence."[1]

Chief Joseph of the beleaguered Nez Perce declared a century later a comparable ethos of governance to "treat all men alike," but the outcome of the spirit of that common native sentiment of liberty was already maligned with cultural mockery and religious abuse and corrupted by colonial empires and a constitutional democracy. William Apess, George Copway, Black Elk, Charles Eastman, Luther Standing Bear, John Rogers, and many other early native authors might have written that it was the cause of native sovereignty and continental liberty that made them authors of survivance in America.

Paine argued in the *Rights of Man*, "Sovereignty, as a matter of right, appertains to the Nation only, and not to any individual," yet he seemed to envy the singularity of native cultures. "The life of an Indian," he observed, "is a continual holiday, compared with the poor of Europe."[2] Chief Joseph, the spirited diplomat and political leader, visited Washington DC in January 1879, more than a century after the inspired vision of Thomas Paine, to argue for tribal recognition and the return of the exiled Nez Perce to their homeland in the Pacific Northwest. Members of Congress, the Cabinet, diplomats, and commercial leaders listened to a memorable, heartfelt entreaty for ordinary justice and liberty.

"If the white man wants to live in peace with the Indian he can live in peace," said Chief Joseph:

> There need be no trouble. Treat all men alike. Give them all the same law. Give them all an even chance to grow. All men were made by the same Great Spirit Chief. They are all brothers. The earth is the mother of all people, and all people should have equal rights upon it. You might as well expect the rivers to run backward as that any man who was born a free man should be contented not penned up and denied liberty to go where he pleases.
>
> When I think of our condition my heart is heavy. I see men of my race treated as outlaws and driven from country to country, or shot down like animals. I know that my race must change. We cannot hold our own with the white men as we are. We only ask an even chance to live as other men live. We ask to be recognized as men. We ask that the same law shall work on all men.[3]

Continental Liberty

Seven years later, on Thursday, March 25, 1886, the first independent newspaper was published on the White Earth Reservation in Minnesota. "The novelty of a newspaper published upon this reservation may cause many to be wary in their support, and this from a fear that it may be revolutionary in character," announced Theodore Beaulieu, the Anishinaabe editor of *The Progress.* "We shall aim to advocate constantly . . . what in our view, and in the view of the leading minds upon this reservation, is the best for the interests of its residents."[4]

T. J. Sheehan, the malevolent United States Indian agent, confiscated the press and ordered the editor and publisher removed from the reservation. The nasty agent would not tolerate "freedom of the press" on the reservation without his specific approval. The Indian agent announced that *The Progress* published "false and malicious statements concerning the affairs of the White Earth Reservation, done evidently for the purpose of breaking down the influence of the United States Indian Agent with the Indians."[5]

The second issue of *The Progress* was published more than a year later on October 8, 1887, after a government investigation, extensive testimony, and a favorable hearing in federal district court. *The Progress* was the first newspaper seized by federal agents in violation of the First Amendment of the United States Constitution.

The United States Supreme Court landmark decision on the freedom of the press was delivered more than forty years later in *Near v. Minnesota,* 1931. The court rejected "prior restraint" censorship of the press. J. M. Near published *The Saturday Press,* a newspaper of racist hatred. The case was based on a state statute that allowed courts to censor malicious and scandalous newspapers.

I was a journalist fifty years ago at the *Minneapolis Tribune.* Frank Premack, the intrepid city editor at the time, shouted his standard advice across the newsroom, "The second com-ing of Christ is worth a page and a half in this newspaper." Let that be a guide to you as a journalist.

I was working on a story about reservation economic development on the Red Lake Reservation, many years before the fantasies of casinos, when Premack left an urgent message for me at the motel in Bemidji, Minnesota. He assigned me to cover the funeral for Dane Michael White the next morning in Sisseton, South Dakota, at least four hours away by car. I arrived in time for the morning service and funeral procession.

Dane White died by suicide almost a century after the emotive entreaty by Chief Joseph. The lonesome Dakota boy never had a chance to envision liberty or a cause to be an author in America. He was held alone in the Wilkin County jail for more than a month on the nominal charge of public school truancy, not a crime, and hanged himself with a wide belt.

I filed my page and a half story that morning by telephone. "Kin, Friends Attend Rites for Young Indian," was published the following day on the front page of the *Minneapolis Tribune*, November 21, 1968.

Sisseton, South Dakota:

Catholic funeral services for Dane White were held here in English and the Dakota language at Saint Catherine's Indian Mission Church. Following the services, attended by seventy-five people, all but six of whom were Dakota Indians, Dane was buried here in Saint Peter's Catholic Cemetery.

Born in Sisseton thirteen years ago, he took his own life Sunday in the Wilkin County Jail, Breckenridge, Minnesota, where he had been held since October 7 awaiting a juvenile court hearing.

The services and burial for the young Dakota Indian were attended by his father, Cyrus White, Browns Valley, Minnesota; his mother, Burdell Armell, Chicago, Illinois; his maternal and paternal grandparents; his older brother,

Timothy, fifteen; three younger sisters, Jodi, twelve, Joan, eleven, and Mary, nine, and many of his school friends.

The Reverend William Keohane conducted the service. Two hymns were sung in the Dakota language. "Dane is here, in the background of the banquet table. Lord remember Dane in your Kingdom," said Father Keohane in prayer, pointing to the large painting of the Last Supper behind the altar of the small Indian church.

Six of Dane's school friends carried his gray metal coffin from the church. Fifteen cars formed the procession to the cemetery on the edge of town. Following the service at the grave, the six young Indian pallbearers removed their honoring ribbons and placed them on the coffin. A cold Dakota wind blew across the slope of Saint Peter's Cemetery. The six pallbearers were the last to leave the grave.

I visited the county jail and asked the sheriff to leave me alone for a few minutes behind bars. I imagined myself as a truant, and jailed alone in the same way, and that could have easily happened to me at age thirteen.

Dane White was never given the chance to live by the same laws as other men. He might have been inspired with the ideas of Chief Joseph and Thomas Paine. Dane might have contended that the American Revolution intruded on native sovereignty and continental liberty.

Dane surely would have been honored for his respect of elders, especially his grandmother, and if he had not been jailed as a common truant from school, he would have been respected as a native citizen, a teacher with tragic wisdom, or maybe one day a journalist, and motivated to write about natives and survivance in a constitutional democracy.

"A vast responsibility rests on the American people, for it their attention is not soon turned forcibly toward the fate of his fast disappearing red brother, and the American statesmen do not soon make a vast change for the better in their present

Indian policy, our nation will make itself liable, at some future day, to hear the voice of the Great Spirit Creator demanding, 'Cain, where is Abel, thy brother? What has thou done? The voice of thy brother's blood crieth unto me from the ground,'" observed the first Anishinaabe state legislator and historian, William Warren, in the *History of the Ojibway Nation*, published by the Minnesota Historical Society in 1885, eighty-three years before the suicide of Dane Michael White in the Wilkin County Jail.[6]

"Slowly he lifts the heavy stones, a little higher with every sentence," wrote Elias Canetti in *Notes from Hampstead*, "and there is nothing that can redeem him except *his own words*."[7]

[12]

Pretense of Sovereignty

William Lawrence and the *Ojibwe News*

William Lawrence was honored as an athlete in high school, served as a captain in the United States Marine Corps in Vietnam, graduated from law school, then directed an economic development program for several years before he established the *Ojibwe News* in 1988. Four years later, in 1992, he founded the *Native American Press*, then served as the resolute editor and an investigative reporter for the *Native American Press/Ojibwe News* for more than twenty years.

His primary motivation in publishing an independent newspaper dedicated to native issues was to defend the civil rights of natives on reservations and to reveal the pretense of absolute treaty sovereignty. And he never hesitated to denounce the malfeasance and corruption on reservations or to expose the deceit, duplicity, and chicanery of elected native leaders and casino money.

Lawrence pointed out that "no governmental powers are set aside for, granted to, or recognized as existing for Indian tribes" in the United States Constitution. "In fact, no plan was laid out in the Constitution for how to deal with Indian tribes at all, although the United States considered tribes to be under its dominion."[1]

Lawrence was rightly admired for his courage and integrity and his persistence and persuasion as an editor. Most of his detractors were exposed for malfeasance in editorials and later indicted and convicted of serious crimes. Darrell Chip Wadena of the White Earth Reservation, for instance, was convicted in United States District Court for bribery, conspiracy, and embezzlement, and served two years in federal prison. Harold Skip Finn of the Leech Lake Reservation was convicted of corruption and also served time in a federal prison.

Lawrence received the 2003 Minnesota Society of Professional Journalists Freedom of Information Award in recognition of his editorial dedication to native rights and the freedom of information, after fifteen years as an editor and investigative reporter. He was a courageous advocate and plucky editor for the rights of natives on federal reservations, and he carried out his advocacy in the great tradition of *The Progress* and later *The Tomahawk*, the first two independent native newspapers published by Augustus Hudon Beaulieu on the White Earth Reservation in Minnesota. The federal agent ordered the removal of the publisher and editor, Theodore Hudon Beaulieu, both native citizens of the reservation, and arbitrarily confiscated the actual rotary press. The second edition of the newspaper was published more than a year later after a federal court decided in favor of the publisher and editor to publish a newspaper on the reservation, or anywhere in in the United States.

The first edition of *The Progress*, March 25, 1886, declared on the front page, "We shall aim to advocate constantly and withhold reserve, what in our view, and in the view of the leading minds upon this reservation, is the best for the interests of the residents. And not only for their interests, but those of the tribe wherever they now are residing."[2] Lawrence carried out a similar stouthearted declaration and much more in his advocacy for native rights on treaty reservations, his investigative reports, and his weekly editorial commentaries of the *Native American Press/Ojibwe News*.

Most native newspapers were initiated and sponsored by reservation governments. Obviously the underwriters managed the news and easily censored critical stories about federal policies, contracts, or most recently the management and distribution of money from casinos.

The *Red Lake Times* was initiated and managed by Roger Jourdain, the notorious elected chairman of the Red Lake Band of Chippewa, but after a year of crude content constraints the newspaper was unreadable and any semblance of unbiased news was dead. The demand for impartial news about reservation politics, however, did not end, and two former writers from the *Red Lake Times* contacted Lawrence to publish a new and independent weekly newspaper named the *Ojibwe News*.

Mike Mosedale reported in *City Pages*, "From the outset, the *Ojibwe News* was an in-your-face publication—or, more accurately, an in-Roger Jourdain's-face publication. The first issue, published in May of 1988, led with an exposé of financial shenanigans at Red Lake. Subsequent editions featured similar stories, along with stinging editorials authored by Lawrence denouncing everyone from the 'dictatorial' Jourdain (and 'his ten little Indians' on the tribal council) to the bureaucrats" of the Bureau of Indian Affairs.[3]

Lawrence conveyed a casual manner of confidence, not courtly or suave but free and easy, learned, always cordial, and with a great sense of native humor and irony. His friends recognized a signature smile that preceded a tease, a familiar native practice in most communities. And, of course, he could easily tease his own serious moments to share a story with a generous sense of humor. He teased me many times, as an activist, a journalist, and as a private in the army and a poet. I counterteased him as a spit and polish officer in the Marine Corps and as a manly muckraker of reservation hucksters. Sometimes he would counter the tease of muckraker with an ironic gesture that Chip Wadena, who was convicted of embezzlement, money laundering, and other crimes, only diverted casino money because he had a huge family to support. Other natives continued the intended irony and characterized Chip Wadena as the Robin Hood of White Earth. The tease countered the medieval legend because the tribal outlaw stole from the losers, the game money at the casino, and seldom shared the loot with the native poor.

Lawrence named the malfeasance "Chippygate."

Mosedale pointed out: "Lawrence is unapologetic. 'We're an advocacy newspaper. People know that. But at least we're independent.' He points out that a vast majority of Indian newspapers are owned outright by the tribes, and that results in muted criticism. 'I don't recognize them as newspapers. They're company papers. They're just gonna print what they're told to print.'"

Lawrence actually "stands in contrast to his maverick sensibilities and sometimes inflammatory rhetoric." He "seldom raises his voice, instead offering his complaints as though he were reading a grocery list aloud."[4]

David Lillehaug, the United States Attorney for Minnesota, for instance, told Mosedale that Lawrence came to his office in Saint Paul and said, "I'm here to tell you there's a serious problem with corruption on Indian reservations in Minnesota, and that I and my publication hope and expect that you will make that a high priority. And if you don't, we will point that out." Lillehaug recalled that Lawrence was obviously forward, but "he didn't come in with a grudge or assuming that he wouldn't be listened to. We hit it off pretty well."

Mosedale pointed out, "For all the criticism he has taken from tribal officials and other members of the Indian establishment, Lawrence has also won the respect—sometimes grudging, sometimes effusive—of dissidents and skeptics, both on and off the reservation. Minnesota Appeals Court Judge Jim Randall, who still remembers Lawrence as a high school athlete, finally met the publisher face-to-face in 1996, after he published a dissent in *Cohen v. Six*."

Lawrence was impressed with Judge Jim Randall, who had questioned the notion of absolute tribal sovereignty and argued that natives on federal reservations were denied the civil rights of ordinary citizens. Reservation governments were not obligated to provide the same civil rights and protections of the Constitution of the United States.

Judge Randall told Mosedale that Lawrence arrived at his courthouse chambers with no notice and said, "I'm Bill Lawrence, publisher of the *Native American Press*, and I've been waiting for your opinion for 28 years." Those who heard and then read the story in *City Pages* were not surprised because the editor and the judge had expressed similar concerns about native civil right and critiques of treaty reservation sovereignty.

Lawrence had read about Judge Randall's dissent to an appeals court decision that Sylvia Cohen, who was not native, should have the right to pursue a case for personal injuries against the Mystic Lake Casino. Mosedale wrote that Judge Randall and Lawrence "shared the same birthday, they are both ex-Marines, both love sports, and both had concluded the notion of tribal sovereignty was a sham." Randall told Mosedale, "The more I learned about what he was doing, how he feels, the more I became convinced that he was on the right track. And he has the clearest mind of any writer working today on what are the problems in Indian country."[5]

Lawrence argued in "In Defense of Indian Rights" that treaties with natives "were *not* solemn promises to preserve in perpetuity historic tribal lifestyles, lands, or cultures, as is often claimed today. In fact, plans for assimilating Indian people into mainstream American life were spelled out in most treaties, often requiring that treaty payments be used for construction of schools, homes, programs to train Indian adults in agriculture, and promises to aide the transition from a subsistence lifestyle to active citizenship." Moreover, he wrote, "Rather than being an indication that tribes were sovereign, many treaties specifically noted the lack of tribal sovereignty, and through treaties, many individual Indians and even entire tribes became" citizens of the United States.[6]

Lawrence was born on the Red Lake Reservation and graduated from Bemidji State University with a degree in business administration. He was a Marine Corps officer in Vietnam, then returned to law school, but interrupted his studies a second time to become the first industrial and economic development officer for the Red Lake Reservation.

He had developed an impressive and ambitious five-year economic and industrial development program for the reservation that concentrated mostly on private enterprise or entrepreneurialism. The program proposed, for instance, a native owned liquor store, motel, restaurants, service station, fuel oil distributor, and larger developments of a golf course and reservation water and power companies.

In a few months' time, Lawrence had obtained federal funds to establish a bulk fuel oil dealership, an industrial park on the reservation, improvements in telephone services and communications, reforestation programs, construction of a utility building, and home construction. Moreover, he sponsored a native entrepreneur to obtain a small business loan from the federal government to build the very first coin-operated laundromat on the reservation. Previously natives had traveled about thirty miles to use automatic washers in Bemidji, Minnesota.

Lawrence was determined to create an economic system independent of the federal government and to support entrepreneurial services that would provide a basic exchange of money, goods, and services on the reservation. Some of these practical entrepreneurial developments, however, were sidetracked by the autocratic leaders of the reservation and the favors of nasty politics.

Roger Jourdain, the elected chairman of the Red Lake Reservation government, was more responsive to outside corporate operations that would exploit native labor and reduce the number of people unemployed. These distinct economic and political philosophies, native entrepreneurs and limited partnerships, and the corporate inducements and exploitation of reservation labor were never easily reconciled in an authoritarian government.

Lawrence was educated and determined to change the reservation government from authoritarian to egalitarian and improve the conditions of dependency and poverty. He decided to enter politics and ran for chairman of the reservation. Roger Jourdain defeated Lawrence and was elected to his fourth term. The politics of favoritism continued, and the enthusiasm for changes in the economic development were diverted to corporate and federal dominance. Jourdain was beholden to his good friends Hubert Humphrey and Walter Mondale and the political favors of the Democratic Farmer Labor Party.

Jourdain had also defeated Leon Cook, another young native who was born on the Red Lake Reservation. Cook wanted to return to the reservation as a progressive chairman with promises of economic change. Cook, like Lawrence, wanted to move aggressively for independent economic development to reduce the dependency on the federal government. Natives on the reservation, however, apparently were not ready for change. There were no distinct party lines in the reservation election, or a clear division of political factions. The arguments and ideas were usually between the old and new favors and promises and between the younger and the older candidates. Lawrence and Cook were the new, young, and educated, and Jourdain was established as the old and familiar, the dole-out contender with reliable favors, and he was the most traditional of the candidates.

Lawrence announced in a press release that he had decided to become a candidate for chairman "so that the Red Lake people will have a clear choice between the dictatorial and irresponsible leadership that presently exists, and the leadership that would frugally and conscientiously manage tribal affairs and be responsible to the people's needs." And "the people of the reservation deserve a better fate than we are now enduring." He clearly conveyed that natives must trust the energy and counsel of the younger educated natives as well as the older tribal members on the reservation. "The people are afraid of change," he said, and "they know most of the time what they can expect from Jourdain."

The *Minneapolis Tribune* described the election as a "contest between those who have stayed on the sprawling community held reservation and those who have left to seek their fortunes in white urban society."[7]

Lawrence was always forthright about an ethos of egalitarian governance and advocated for the democratic doctrine of a balance of power on reservations, and these concepts of governance were the necessary revisions in native constitutions and reservation governments. He directed native education programs for several years, and continued his dedication to reservation government reform and advocacy of native civil rights as an investigative journalist, editor, and publisher of the *Native American Press/Ojibwe News.*

Lawrence was a steadfast advocate of native rights, and he pointed out that the "underlying problem is that true democracy does not exist on Indian reservations. Tribal elections are often not free and fair elections, and typically they are not monitored by any third party." He argued that true democracy "includes more than just the presence of an election process. Democracy is also defined by limiting the power of the government by such things as the rule of law, separation of powers, checks on the power of each branch of government, equality under the law, impartial courts, *due* process, and protection of the basic liberties of speech, assembly, press, and property."[8]

I was a staff writer for the *Minneapolis Tribune* at the time and prepared a series of articles on the problems of economic development on native reservations in Minnesota. Lawrence was clearly the most dedicated, educated, and articulate about economic development on the Red Lake Reservations. Our friendship started with several days of conversations about the exchange of money, goods and services, and entrepreneurs on the reservation. I wrote articles about these issues for the *Minneapolis Tribune* and later wrote about native economic development programs in a special research report for the Federal Reserve Bank in Minneapolis and about the same time in the early 1970s in my book *The Everlasting Sky: New Voices from the People Named the Chippewa.*

"I am proud of my heritage as a member of the Red Lake Band, and share the desire for the Indian people to preserve their languages, their cultures, their customs and their traditions. But in a world of accelerating change globally, to believe that the Indian people can isolate themselves on small parcels of land on this earth and defy the winds of change is a prescription for economic failure and cultural elimination," Lawrence wrote in an editorial entitled *Do Indian Reservations Equal Apartheid?* His critical comments were both personal and ironic, of course, that natives "have no access to federal courts for redress of wrongs done to them by tribal government. Because tribal government all too often controls the tribal courts, directly, or through the power of appropriations, there is no oversight and control of tribal councils. The result is rampant, continuous and ongoing problems with corruption, abuse, violence or discord. Most tribes do not give their members audited financial statements of tribal funds or casino funds, which may represent thousands of dollars per tribal member. It is literally impossible for tribal members to find out where all of the money is going."

Lawrence continued his editorial of critical assessments about the politics of separatism and federal funding as a response to the comments of Gene Merriam, commissioner of the Department of Natural Resources in Minnesota who stated, "any system of apartheid based on race is inherently misdirected." Lawrence declared, "The fact is that the federal government created Indian reservations in this country which were designed to separate people by race. There is a serious question whether tribal governments were truly offended by the use of the term 'apartheid.'" Despite

> expenditures of millions of dollars annually by the federal and state governments, the problems of poverty, lack of economic opportunity, poor graduation rates, chemical dependency, serious health problems and unacceptable crime rates have not been solved.
>
> Tribal governments were created by constitutions imposed upon the various Indian bands and tribes by the Bureau of Indian Affairs. Then the federal government washed its hands of tribal governments. . . . In most tribal constitutions there is no separation of powers. All power, legislative, executive, and judicial, is concentrated in or controlled by the tribal council. James Madison, a founding father of the United States Constitution, described the accumulation of all of these powers in the same hands as "the very definition of tyranny." The sad truth is that true democracy does not exist on most Indian reservations. Tribal elections are often not free and fair.[9]

William Lawrence wrote his last editorial column, "A Warrior's Creed: Today Is a Good Day to Die," and closed *the Native American Press/Ojibwe News* on September 1, 2009. "This is the most difficult assignment I've faced in twenty-one years of publishing," Lawrence wrote in the Editorial and Commentary page. He continued, "There is much I want to say. The question is how much of it is now relevant and meaningful. Then there's the unpleasant fact that these will be my last words, editorially speaking. There will be no possibility for corrections, further explanation or apology." Lawrence revealed that circulation had declined in the past few years, many advertisers had turned to internet sites, and he was dying of prostate cancer. Still, "given the situation of our

Pretense of Sovereignty

local reservations, we served an important service in shining a light on the black deeds of those in power."

Lawrence continued in his last commentary,

Doubly disappointing is the on-going and increasing violence, crime and oppression on reservations. Despite appeals by the people, the Federal government refused to step in to restore order.

Lastly, we are saddened to realize that we offered a forum for the people to speak out and they have mostly chosen not to do so. They have chosen instead to hunker down and take whatever comes along. I regret that I haven't been able to convince tribes of the benefits of democracy. They live in a country that is a role model for many other nations in the world and yet do not avail themselves of its benefits.[10]

William Lawrence died on March 2, 2010, of prostate cancer at the Veterans Affairs Medical Center in Boise, Idaho. Roxanne Jensen, his loving companion, said, "He just died very quietly and gently, as he had lived." She pointed out that his cancer had already advanced when he was diagnosed in March 2008, more than a year before he wrote his last editorial column.[11]

Diane White wrote on the front page of the last issue, "Farewell to the *Native American Press/Ojibwe News*," that for more than twenty years the independent newspaper was "dedicated to our Indian communities throughout Minnesota." She closed her column with a gesture to the next generation of writers and publishers. "Good luck. It is a wonderful, sometimes scary world to journey in, especially if you uncover corruption and dirty politicians."[12]

[ENVOY]

Native Provenance: The Betrayal of Cultural Creativity is a collection of twelve original essays based on shorter versions of keynote lectures, special seminars, articles in journals, and presentations at international conferences primarily in the past decade in France, Germany, Austria, England, Canada, Japan, and the United States.

The first essay, "Gossip Theory," is an expansion and critical elaboration of my concise Berkhofer Lecture at the University of Michigan in March 2018 and a similar concise essay published as "Native American Irony: Survivance and the Subversion of Ethnology" in *Race and Cultural Practice in Popular Culture* published by Rutgers University Press, 2019.

The references to Ishi, the Yahi Native American, were reconstructed and expanded from a dedication presentation of Ishi Court and a commencement lecture for the Division of Undergraduate and Interdisciplinary Studies at the University of California, Berkeley, in May 2008.

"Survivance and Liberty" was published as an essay in a shorter version in a special issue of *Revue Française d'Études Américaines*, "Les nations de l'intérieur: The Nations Within," Paris, France, 2015.

The essay "Native Transmotion" was expanded from a conference lecture at Kings College, London, in May 2014. An earlier version of the essay, "The Unmissable: Transmotion in Native American Stories and Literature," was published as the inaugural essay in *Transmotion*, an online journal, and included more examples of visionary motion in native literature and in *Moby-Dick* by Herman Melville.

"Natives of the Progressive Era" originated as a more concise keynote lecture at a conference at the University of Flensburg, Germany, and was published as "Standing Bear and Karl May: Authors of the Progressive Era" in a special issue of the journal *Literatur in Wissenschaft und Unterricht*, "Teaching Native Literatures and Cultures in Europe," edited by Birgit Däwes and Kristina Baudemann, in 2016.

Two shorter versions of "Expeditions in France" were presented as lectures at the British Library in London and at Amerika Haus, Vienna, Austria, in June 2014. A shorter version of the essay was published in *Native American Survivance, Memory, and Futurity: The Gerald Vizenor Continuum*, edited by Birgit Däwes and Alexandra Hauke and published by Routledge in 2017. A similar essay, "Empire Treasons: White Earth and the Great War," was presented at Globalizing the Word: Transnationalism and the Making of Native American Literature, a conference at the University of Michigan, May 2013. A more elaborate version of the essay "Expeditions in France" was published as "Empire Treasons: White Earth and the Great War" in *The World, the Text, and the Indian*, edited by Scott Richard Lyons and published by SUNY Press in 2017.

The essay "Visionary Sovereignty" was presented as a concise lecture at the Universitat de València, Spain, and published in *Literary Chance: Essays on Native American Survivance* in the series Biblioteca Javier Coy d'estudis nord-americans in 2007.

"Cosmototemic Art" was a shorter conference lecture and published in *Sakahàn*, an exhibition of native art at the National Gallery of Canada, Ottawa, May 2013. The essay included theoretical ideas from a lecture at a symposium of the *Sakahàn* exhibition at the National Gallery of Canada in the same year. "Native *Nouveau Roman*" was greatly expanded from a panel lecture at the United Nations Educational, Scientific, and Cultural Organization in Paris, 2010. The original title of the shorter lecture and essay, "Survivance et sagesse tragique: La littérature des peuples autochtones d'Amérique du nord," or "American Indian Art and Literature Today: Survivance and Tragic Wisdom," was published by the United Nations. "Native *Nouveau Roman*" considers critical theory and comparative literature, including a discussion of natural motion in *Moby-Dick* by Herman Melville based on my lecture "Ishmael Ashore in Hiroshima," presented at Keio University, Tokyo, Japan, October 2004.

"Time Warp Provenance" is an essay based on a much shorter lecture presented at a symposium held at the Smithsonian National Museum of the American Indian in Washington, February 2007. The essay includes a discussion of native artists from several other seminar lectures in the past few years.

"Trickster Hermeneutics" has been expanded with a wider discussion of literature and critical theory from a special seminar lecture presented at the University of Geneva, Switzerland, in 2006.

"Continental Liberty" is a revision and expansion of a concise commencement lecture at Bemidji State University on occasion of my being named a recipient of the Distinguished Minnesota Award in May 2005.

"Pretense of Sovereignty" is an expanded essay first prepared in a shorter form as the introduction to an edited collection of editorial articles by William Lawrence, the editor and publisher of the *Native American Press/Ojibwe News*.

[NOTES]

1. Gossip Theory

1. Thomas Thorowgood, *Jewes in America, or Probabilities, That the Americans Are Jewes* (London: Henry Brome at the Gun in Ivie-Lane, 1660) 3, 6, available in the New York Public Library Digital Collection, http://digitalcollections.nypl.org/items/8c527043-06dc-15a6-e040-e00a180659d7, and Oliver's Bookshelf, http://olivercowdery.com/texts/1650Thor.htm.

2. Avishai Margalit, *On Betrayal* (Cambridge: Harvard University Press, 2017), 74, 83.

3. "Irony," *The New Shorter Oxford English Dictionary*, vol. 1 (Oxford: Clarendon Press, 1993), 1417.

4. Frances Densmore, *Chippewa Music* (Washington DC: Government Printing Office, 1910, 1913; repr. Minneapolis: Ross and Haines, 1973), 88, 89; Gerald Vizenor, *Summer in the Spring* (Norman: University of Oklahoma Press, 1993), 55, 152, 153.

5. Vine Deloria Jr., *Custer Died for Your Sins* (New York: Macmillan, 1969), 146, 147.

6. Gerald Vizenor, "Native Tease: Narratives of Irony and Survivance," in *Literary Chance: Essays on Native American Survivance*, ed. Gerald Vizenor (València, Spain: Universitat de València, 2007), 79, 80.

7. Vizenor, *Literary Chance*, 80. Also, Gerald Vizenor, *The People Named the Chippewa: Narrative Histories* (Minneapolis: University of Minnesota Press, 1984) 8, 9.

8. Michael Silverstein, "Of Two Minds About Minding Language in Culture," in *Indigenous Visions: Rediscovering the World of Franz Boas*, ed. Ned Blackhawk and Isaiah Lorado Wilner (New Haven: Yale University Press, 2018), 147.

9. Franz Boas, *The Mind of Primitive Man* (New York: Macmillan, 1911, 1922), 244, 248.

10. Franz Boas and J. W. Powell, Introduction to *Handbook of American Indian Languages and Linguistic Families of America North of Mexico*, new ed. (Lincoln: University of Nebraska Press, 2017), 5, 6.

11. Michael Silverstein, Introduction to *Handbook of American Indian Languages*, xv.

12. Michael Silverstein, "Language Culture and Linguistic Ideology," *The Elements: A Parasession on Linguistic Units and Levels*, ed. Paul R. Clyne, William F. Hanks, and Carol L Hofbauer (Chicago: Chicago Linguistic Society, University of Chicago, 1979), 193.

13. "Sapir-Whorf Hypothesis," Anthropology, iResearchNet, April 26, 2018, http://anthropology.iresearchnet.com/sapir-whorf-hypothesis/.

14. Judith Irvine, "Language Ideology," *Oxford Bibliographies*, April 21, 2018, http://www.oxfordbibliographies.com/view/document/obo-9780199766567/obo-9780199766567-0012.xml.

15. Michael Silverstein, "'Cultural' Concepts and the Language-Culture Nexus," *Current Anthropology* 45, no. 5 (December 2004): 621, 622.

16. Stuart Sim, *Derrida and the End of History* (New York: Totem Books, 1999), 33, 71.

17. Clifford Geertz, *The Interpretation of Cultures* (New York: Basic Books, 1973), 7, 10.

18. Charles Dickens, *American Notes* (New York: Random House, Modern Library Edition, 1966) 327.

19. Dickens, *American Notes*, 219.

20. Dickens, *American Notes*, 302.

21. M. H. Dunlop, *Sixty Miles from Contentment: Traveling the Nineteenth-Century American Interior* (New York: Basic Books, 1995), 113.

22. Mary Ashe Miller, "Indian Enigma Is Study for Scientists," *San Francisco Call*, September 6, 1911; Robert Heizer and Theodora Kroeber, *Ishi the Last Yahi: A Documentary History* (Berkeley: University of California Press, 1979), 97.

23. Theodora Kroeber, *Alfred Kroeber: A Personal Configuration* (Berkeley: University of California Press, 1970), 81.

24. Grant Wallace, "Ishi, the Last Aboriginal Savage in America, Finds Enchantment in a Vaudeville Show," *San Francisco Call*, October 8, 1911; Heizer and Kroeber, *Ishi the Last Yahi*, 107.

25. Saxton Pope, *The Medical History of Ishi* (Berkeley: University of California Publications in American Archaeology and Ethnology, 1920); Heizer and Kroeber, *Ishi the Last Yahi*, 107.

26. Wallace, "Ishi"; Heizer and Kroeber, *Ishi the Last Yahi*, 108.

27. Theodora Kroeber, *Ishi in Two Worlds* (Berkeley: University of California Press, 1961), 236.

28. "Naming Ceremony," *California Magazine*, March/April 2007, 29.

29. Jonathan Lear, *A Case for Irony* (Cambridge: Harvard University Press, 2011), 9, 15, 18, 19, 42, 43.

30. Victor Barnouw, *Wisconsin Chippewa Myths and Tales* (Madison: University of Wisconsin Press, 1977), 4, 6, 13, 68.

31. Dennis Tedlock, *The Spoken Word and the Work of Interpretation* (Philadelphia: University of Pennsylvania Press, 1983), 15, cited in Gerald Vizenor, "Trickster Discourse: Comic Holotropes and Language Games," in *Narrative Chance*, ed. Gerald Vizenor (Albuquerque: University of New Mexico Press, 1989) 200.

32. Barnouw, *Wisconsin Chippewa Myths*, 240, 241.

33. Barnouw, *Wisconsin Chippewa Myths*, 54.

34. Alan Dundas, "Earth-Diver: Creation of the Mythopoeic Male," *American Anthropologist*, 1962: 64, reprinted in *Sacred Narrative*, ed. Alan Dundas (Berkeley: University of California Press, 1984), 278.

35. "National Poo Museum Exhibits Encourage Excitement for Excrement," United Press International, April 4, 2016, http://www.upi.com/Odd_News/2016/04/04/National-Poo-Museum-exhibits-encourage-excitement-for-excrement/1131459795278/.

2. Survivance and Liberty

1. Gilles Harvard, *The Great Peace of Montreal of 1701*, trans. Phyllis Aronoff and Howard Scott (Montréal: McGill-Queen's University Press, 2001), 111.

2. Harvard, *Great Peace*, 28.

3. Harvard, *Great Peace*, 21.

4. Harvard, *Great Peace*, 180.

5. Stuart Banner, *How the Indians Lost Their Land: Law and Power on the Frontier* (Cambridge: Harvard University Press, 2005), 14, 16.

6. Banner, *How the Indians Lost Their Land*, 40.

7. David E. Wilkins, "Sovereignty, Democracy, Constitution: An Introduction," in Gerald Vizenor and Jill Doerfler, *The White Earth Nation: Ratification of a Native Democratic Constitution* (Lincoln: University of Nebraska Press, 2012), 2.

8. W. J. Eccles, *The Canadian Frontier, 1534–1760* (New York: Holt, Rinehart and Winston, 1969; repr., Albuquerque: University of New Mexico Press, 1983), 110.

9. Banner, *How the Indians Lost Their Land*, 247.

10. Banner, *How the Indians Lost Their Land*, 249, 250.

11. N. Bruce Duthu, *Shadow Nations: Tribal Sovereignty and the Limits of Legal Pluralism* (Oxford University Press, 2013), 44, 45.

12. David Bromwich, *Moral Imagination: Essays* (Princeton University Press, 2014), xii.

13. Wilkins, "Sovereignty, Democracy, Constitution," 7.

14. Jacques Rancière, *Hatred of Democracy* (London: Verso, 2006), 6.

15. Daniel Nelson, *An Honor Roll: Containing a Pictorial Record of the Men and Women from Becker County* (Detroit: D. Nelson, 1920), 4, available at http://babel.hathitrust.org/cgi/pt?id=wu.89066170879;view=1up;seq=9. Nelson compiled and published biographical notes about soldiers and nurses who served in the American Expeditionary Forces in the First World War. Detroit, the original name of the city and township, was changed to Detroit Lakes, Minnesota, on September 7, 1926.

16. Thomas A. Britten, *American Indians in World War I* (Albuquerque: University of New Mexico Press, 1977), 38.

17. Gerald Vizenor, *Survivance: Narratives of Native Presence* (Lincoln: University of Nebraska Press, 2008), 1–23.

18. Gerald Vizenor, *Fugitive Poses: Native American Indian Scenes of Absence and Presence* (Lincoln: University of Nebraska Press, 1998), 167–69.

3. Native Transmotion

1. Gerald Vizenor, *Fugitive Poses: Native American Indian Scenes of Absence and Presence* (Lincoln: University of Nebraska Press, 1998), 15.

2. Gerald Vizenor, *Native Liberty: Natural Reason and Cultural Survivance* (Lincoln: University of Nebraska Press, 2009), 1, 162.

3. John D. Nichols and Earl Nyholm, *A Concise Dictionary of Minnesota Ojibwe* (Minneapolis: University of Minnesota Press, 1995).

4. Frances Densmore, *Chippewa Music*, vol. 1 (Minneapolis: Ross and Haines, 1973), 204.

5. Frances Densmore, *Chippewa Music*, vol. 2 (Minneapolis: Ross and Haines, 1973), 254.

6. Densmore, *Chippewa Music*, 1:134.

7. Densmore, *Chippewa Music*, 1:15.

8. Kobayashi Issa, *The Year of My Life: A Translation of Issa's* Oragu Haru, trans. Nobuyaki Yuasa (Berkeley: University of California Press, 1960), 103, 104.

9. Stephen Addiss, *The Art of Haiku* (Boston: Shambhala, 2012), 260.

10. Toni Jensen, "At the Powwow Hotel," in Toni Jensen, *From the Hilltop* (Lincoln: University of Nebraska Press, 2010), 55, 56, 57.

11. Jensen, *From the Hilltop*, 67.

12. Leslie Marmon Silko, *Ceremony* (New York: Viking Penguin, 1977), 132, 133.

13. Gerald Vizenor, *Shrouds of White Earth* (Albany: State University of New York Press, 2010), 3, 5, 6.

14. Diane Glancy, *Designs of the Night Sky* (Lincoln: University of Nebraska Press, 2002), 5; Gerald Vizenor, ed., *Native Storiers: Five Selections* (Lincoln: University of Nebraska Press, 2009).

15. N. Scott Momaday, *The Way to Rainy Mountain* (Albuquerque: University of New Mexico Press, 1969), 7. A fuller discussion was published in Gerald Vizenor, *Manifest Manners: Narratives on Postindian Survivance* (Lincoln: University of Nebraska Press, 1994), 57.

16. Gerald Vizenor and Jill Doerfler, *The White Earth Nation: Ratification of a Native Democratic Constitution* (Lincoln: University of Nebraska Press, 2012), 63–79.

17. Gerald Vizenor, "Native Cosmototemic Art," in *Sakahàn: International Art* (Ottawa: National Gallery of Canada, 2013), 50.

18. Rachel Donadio, "Zuni Ask Europe to Return Sacred Art," *New York Times*, April 8, 2014, accessed April 16, 2014, http://www.nytimes.com/2014/04/09/arts/design/zuni-petition-european-museums-to-return-sacred-objects.html?_r=1.

19. John Bryant, "*Moby-Dick* as Revolution," in *The Cambridge Companion to Herman Melville*, ed. Robert S. Levine (Cambridge: Cambridge University Press, 1998), 73.

20. Herman Melville, *Moby-Dick* (New York: W. W. Norton, 1976), 373.

21. Melville, *Moby-Dick*, 374.

22. Melville, *Moby-Dick*, 3.

23. Melville, *Moby-Dick*, 204–5.

24. Melville, *Moby-Dick*, 261, 262.

25. Melville, *Moby-Dick*, 268.

26. Melville, *Moby-Dick*, 447–48.

27. Stephen Zelnick, "*Moby-Dick*: the Republic at Sea," in Herman Melville, *Moby-Dick*, ed. Mary R. Reichardt (San Francisco: Ignatius Press, 2011), 691, 703.

28. Bryant, "*Moby-Dick* as Revolution," 70.

29. Bryant, "*Moby-Dick* as Revolution," 72.

30. Vizenor, *Native Liberty*, 1, 162.

4. Natives of the Progressive Era

1. "Indian Citizenship Act, President Coolidge and Osage Indians Photograph, 1924," Shaping the Constitution, Library of Virginia, accessed December 8, 2018, http://edu.lva.virginia.gov/online_classroom/shaping_the_constitution/doc/indian_citizenship_act.

2. Rivka Galchen, "Wild West Germany," *New Yorker*, April 9, 2012, accessed July 12, 2016, http://www.newyorker.com/magazine/2012/04/09/wild-west-germany.

3. Galchen, "Wild West Germany," 7.

4. Christian F. Feest, "Indians and Europe? Editor's Postscript," in *Indians and Europe*, ed. Christian F. Feest (Lincoln: University of Nebraska Press, 1989), 620.

5. Karl May, *Winnetou: The Chief of the Apache*, trans. Mary A. Thomas, Kindle ed. (Liverpool: CTPDC Publishing, 2014).

6. Feest, "Indians and Europe?," 622.

7. Julia Simone Stetler, "Buffalo Bill's Wild West in Germany" (PhD diss., University of Nevada, Las Vegas, 2006), 285, 286, accessed July 12, 2016, http://digitalscholarship.unlv.edu/cgi/viewcontent.cgi?article=2635&context =thesesdissertations.

8. Stetler, "Buffalo Bill's Wild West," 286.

9. Jan Fleischhauer, "Germany's Best-Loved Cowboy: The Fantastical World of Cult Novelist Karl May," *Spiegel Online International*, March 30, 2012, accessed July 14, 2016, http://www.spiegel.de/international/germany /marking-the-100th-anniversary-of-german-cult-author-karl-may-s-death -a-824566.html.

10. Stuart Banner, *How the Indians Lost Their Land: Law and Power on the Frontier* (Cambridge: Harvard University Press, 2005), 249.

11. Stetler, "Buffalo Bill's Wild West," 174.

12. Daniele Florentino, "'Those Red-Brick Faces': European Press Reactions to the Indians of Buffalo Bill's Wild West Show," in Feest, *Indians and Europe*, 408.

13. William S. E. Coleman, *Voices of Wounded Knee* (Lincoln: University of Nebraska Press, 2000), 123.

14. "Documents Relating to the Wounded Knee Massacre," Digital History, 2016, accessed July 12, 2016, http://www.digitalhistory.uh.edu/disp_textbook .cfm?smtid=3&psid=1101.

15. Galchen, "Wild West Germany," 3.

16. Galchen, "Wild West Germany," 3.

17. L. G. Moses, *Wild West Shows and the Images of American Indians* (Albuquerque: University of New Mexico Press, 1996), 279.

18. Charles Alexander Eastman, *From the Deep Woods to Civilization* (Chicago: R. R. Donnelley and Sons, 2001), 233, 234, 237.

19. Eastman, *From the Deep Woods*, 313.

20. Luther Standing Bear, *My People the Sioux* (1928; repr., Lincoln: University of Nebraska Press, 1975), 223, 224.

21. Standing Bear, *My People the Sioux*, 184, 185.

22. Moses, *Wild West Shows*, 277.

23. Robert E. Bieder, *Science Encounters the Indian, 1820–1880* (Norman: University of Oklahoma Press, 1986), 11, 12.

24. Tiffany Jones Miller, "Eugenics, American Progressivism, and the 'German Idea of the State,'" *Law and Liberty*, January 31, 2013, accessed July 12, 2016, http://www.libertylawsite.org/2013/01/31/eugenics-american-progressivism -and-the-german-idea-of-the-state/.

25. Eastman, *From the Deep Woods*, 189.

5. Expeditions in France

1. Susan Applegate Krouse, *North American Indians in the Great War* (Lincoln: University of Nebraska Press, 2007), 3, 4, 5.

2. Roberta Smith, "Always Outrageous, Frequently Disturbing," *New York Times*, March 12, 2010.

3. Modris Eksteins, "Memory and the Great War," in *The Oxford Illustrated History of the First World War*, ed. Hew Strachan (Oxford: Oxford University Press, 1998), 312.

4. William Warren, *History of the Ojibway Nation* (Saint Paul: Minnesota Historical Society, 1885; repr., Minneapolis: Ross and Haines, 1957), 194, 195.

5. Margaret MacMillan, *The War That Ended Peace* (New York, Random House, 2013), 640.

6. Louis Barthas, *Poilu: The World War I Notebooks* (New Haven: Yale University Press, 2014). First published as *Lex carnets de guerre de Louis Barthas* (Paris: Editions La Découverte, 1978).

7. *The Progress* became *The Tomahawk*, and the number of pages increased with syndicated patent insides of national and international news. For a wider discussion of the independent newspapers on the White Earth Reservation, please see Gerald Vizenor, "Native Liberty," in Gerald Vizenor, *Native Liberty: Natural Reason and Cultural Survivance* (University of Nebraska Press, 2009).

8. David Reynolds, *The Long Shadow* (New York: Simon and Schuster, 2013), 35. Reynolds compared only the dead soldiers, not the actual casualties, which would include the dead, wounded, and missing. The total number of United States and Confederate States dead soldiers in the Civil War battles of Gettysburg, Shiloh, Antietam, and Cold Harbor, was at least 17,000, compared to the 26,000 men killed in action at Meuse-Argonne in October 1918. The Civil War casualties, dead, wounded, and missing at the four battle sites mentioned was more than 110,000. Reynolds did not include the German dead in the battle of Meuse-Argonne.

9. Daniel Nelson, *An Honor Roll: Containing a Pictorial Record of the Men and Women from Becker County* (Detroit: D. Nelson, 1920), 4, available at http://babel.hathitrust.org/cgi/pt?id=wu.89066170879;view=1up;seq=9.

10. Joëlle and Nicolas Rostkowski, owners of the Galerie Orenda in Paris, France, traveled with me and retired justice Gary Strankman to Saint-Quentin, Montbréhain, and Bois du Fays, the actual locations where Ignatius Vizenor and Lawrence Vizenor engaged in combat in October 1918.

11. Gerald Vizenor, *Blue Ravens* (Middletown CT: Wesleyan University Press, 2014), 111, 117.

12. Thomas A. Britten, *American Indians in World War I* (Albuquerque: University of New Mexico Press, 1977), 38; reference to U.S. House of Representatives, *Bill to Raise Ten or More Regiments of Indian Cavalry*, 65th Congress, 1st Session, House Resolution 3970, *Congressional Record* 55, April 30, 1917.

13. Britten, *American Indians*, 44.

14. Diane Camurat, "The American Indian in the Great War: Real and Imagined," (master's thesis, Institute Charles V, University of Paris, 1993), accessed February 15, 2014, http://net.lib.byu.edu/~rdh7/wwi/comment /camurat1.html.

15. President Wilson, General John Pershing, and Secretary of War Newton Baker accommodated the stipulations of southern state racists and the specious notion of "separate but equal" as a policy of segregated military units for African Americans, or the Buffalo Soldiers, in the American Expeditionary Forces in France.

16. Matthew Dennis, *Red, White, and Blue Letter Day* (Ithaca: Cornell University Press, 2005), 66.

17. Britten, *American Indians*, 133.

18. Russell Lawrence Barsh, "American Indians in the Great War," *Ethnohistory* 38, no. 3 (Summer 1991): 277, 278.

19. Britten, *American Indians*, 82.

20. Britten, *American Indians*, 54.

21. Nelson, *An Honor Roll*, 1.

22. Nelson, *An Honor Roll*, 13.

23. Nelson, *An Honor Roll*, 13.

24. Nelson, *An Honor Roll*, 13; "Fred Casebeer," American Battle Monuments Commission, accessed December 8, 2018, https://www.abmc.gov/node /339962#.XAw9Bi3MxuU.

25. Mitchell Yockelson, *Borrowed Soldiers: Americans Under British Command, 1918* (Norman: University of Oklahoma Press, 2008), 190.

26. Robert H. Ferrell, *America's Deadliest Battle* (Lawrence: University of Kansas Press, 2007), 91.

27. Vizenor, *Blue Ravens*, 169, 170.

6. Visionary Sovereignty

1. Thomas Paine, Introduction to *Common Sense*, in *The Writings of Thomas Paine, Volume I, 1774–1779*, collected and edited by Moncure Daniel Conway (New York: G. P. Putnam, 1894), 67, 68.

2. Thomas Paine, *Common Sense and Other Writings* (New York: Modern Library, 2003), 95; National Humanities Center, *The American Crisis* no. 13 (April 19, 1783).

3. Paine, Introduction to *Common Sense*, 69.

4. Thomas Paine, *American Crisis (1780–83)*, 236, available at American History: From Revolution to Reconstruction and Beyond, accessed December 8, 2018, http://www.let.rug.nl/usa/documents/1776-1785/thomas-paine -american-crisis/.

5. Thomas Paine, *Agrarian Justice* (London: W. T. Sherwin, 1817), 5.

6. Colin Calloway, *The World Turned Upside Down: Indian Voices from Early America* (Boston: Bedford/St. Martin's, 1994), 6.

7. Calloway, *World Turned Upside Down*, 7.

8. Samson Occom, Autobiography, Dartmouth College, Occom Circle, Modern Version, Manuscript 1765, 1768, pages 10r, 13v, original manuscript available at https://collections.dartmouth.edu/occom/html/normalized/768517-normalized.html.

9. Joseph Brant, "Brant to Lord George Germaine," Bartleby.com, accessed April 3, 2018, http://www.bartleby.com/268/8/2.html.

10. John Sugden, "Brant, Joseph," *Encyclopedia of North American Indians*, ed. Frederick Hoxie (Boston: Houghton Mifflin, 1996) 85.

11. William Apess, *A Son of the Forest and Other Writings*, edited with an introduction by Barry O'Connell (Amherst: University of Massachusetts Press, 1992, repr. 1997), x, xvii.

12. Apess, *A Son of the Forest*, 31.

13. George Copway, *The Life, History, and Travels of Kah-ge-ga-gah-bowh* (Philadelphia: J. Harmstead, 1847), 155, 156.

14. Thomas Paine, *Selected Writings of Thomas Paine*, ed. Ian Shapiro and Jane Calvert (New Haven: Yale University Press, 2014), 555.

15. Paine, *Selected Writings of Thomas Paine*, 259.

16. Chief Joseph, "An Indian's View of Indian Affairs," *North American Review*, April 1879, 431, 432.

17. T. Alexander Aleinikoff, *Semblances of Sovereignty: The Constitution, The State, and American Citizenship* (Cambridge: Harvard University Press, 2002), 127, 128.

18. John Boli, "Sovereignty from a World Polity Perspective," in *Problematic Sovereignty: Contested Rules and Political Possibilities*, ed. Stephen Krasner (New York: Columbia University Press, 2001), 53, 54, 55.

19. John Collier, "A New Deal for Native Americans," Annual Report of the Secretary of the Interior, 1934, 78, Digital History, accessed April 3, 2018, www.digitalhistory.uh.edu/disp_textbook.cfm?smtid=3&psid=716.

20. John Collier, *Indians of the Americas* (New York: New American Library, 1965), 23.

21. Francis Paul Prucha, *The Indians in American Society* (Berkeley: University of California Press, 1985), 63, 65.

22. Douglas MacArthur, *Reminiscences: General of the Army Douglas MacArthur* (New York: McGraw-Hill, 1964), 282, 283.

7. Cosmototemic Art

1. Gerald Vizenor and Jill Doerfler, *The White Earth Nation: Ratification of a Native Democratic Constitution* (Lincoln: University of Nebraska Press, 2012), 63, 65.

2. David Whitley, Cave Paintings and the Human Spirit (Amherst NY: Prometheus Books, 2009). "The Art of Chauvet Cave," Bradshaw Foundation, September 9, 2012, www.bradshawfoundation.com.

3. Werner Herzog, dir., *Cave of Forgotten Dreams* (documentary film, 2010).

4. Whitley, *Cave Paintings*, 75.

5. Ekkehart Malotki, *The Rock Art of Arizona* (Walnut CA: Kiva Publishing, 2007).

6. Gerald Vizenor, "Aesthetics of Survivance," in Gerald Vizenor, *Native Liberty: Natural Reason and Cultural Survivance* (Lincoln: University of Nebraska Press, 2009), 86, 97.

7. Selwyn Dewdney and Kenneth Kidd, *Indian Rock Paintings of the Great Lakes* (Toronto: University of Toronto Press, 1962), 20.

8. Franz Boas, *Primitive Art* (Mineola NY: Dover Publications, 2010), 64, 88.

9. Wassily Kandinsky, *Concerning the Spiritual in Art* (New York: Dover Publications, 1977), 29. The first translated edition, entitled *The Art of Spiritual Harmony*, was published by Constable and Company Limited in London, 1914. Kandinsky wrote, "A painter, who finds no satisfaction in mere representations, however artistic, in his longing to express his inner life, cannot but envy the ease with which music. . . . achieves this end. He naturally seeks to apply the methods of music to his own art. *So, it is evident that form-harmony must rest only on a corresponding vibration of the human soul; and this is a second guiding principle of the inner need*" (Kandinsky, *Concerning the Spiritual*, 19).

10. Henri Bergson, *Creative Evolution* (New York: Henry Holt, 1911; repr., Mineola NY: Dover Publications, 1998), 103. Bergson observed that if "evolution is a creation unceasingly renewed, it creates, as it goes on, not only the forms of life, but the ideas that will enable the intellect to understand it, the terms which will serve to express it" (103).

11. Ernst H. Gombrich, *The Story of Art* (London: Phaidon Press, 2012), 49. Phaidon Press published the first edition in 1950. There have been sixteen editions of *The Story of Art*.

12. Gombrich, *The Story of Art*, 425.

13. Gombrich, *The Story of Art*, 21.

14. "Oscar Howe, Cubism, and Traditional Native American Art," Archives and Special Collections Blog, University Libraries, University of South Dakota, 2005, accessed September 16, 2012, http://archivesandspecialcollections .wordpress.com/2012/03/23/oscar-howe-cubism-and-traditional-native -american-art/.

15. Gerald Vizenor, "George Morrison," in Vizenor, *Native Liberty*, 207–26.

16. Vizenor, *Native Liberty*, 207.

17. Janet C. Berlo and Ruth B. Phillips, *Native North American Art* (New York: Oxford University Press, 1998), 217.

18. Berlo and Phillips, *Native North American Art*, 217, 223, 225.

19. Phoebe Farris, "Contemporary Native American Women Artists: Visual Expressions of Feminism, the Environment, and Identity," *Feminist Studies* 31, no. 1 (Spring 2005): 107.

20. David McIntosh, Robert Houle exhibition catalogue, *enuhmo andúhyaun, The Road Home*, School Art Gallery, University of Manitoba, September 7 to October 12, 2012.

21. John Murray, *Carl Beam: The Whale of Our Being* (Ottawa: Robert McLaughlin Gallery, 2002), 29.

22. Greg A. Hill, *Carl Beam: The Poetics of Being* (Ottawa: National Gallery of Canada, 2010).

23. Allan J. Ryan, *The Trickster Shift: Humour and Irony in Contemporary Native Art* (Seattle: University of Washington Press, 1999), 151.

24. David P. Becker, "The Visionary Art of Rick Bartow," in *Rick Bartow* (New York: Jamison Thomas Gallery, 1992), 5.

25. Danielle Knapp, "My Life Is Work. Work Is a Blessing!" in *Rick Bartow: Things You Know but Cannot Explain* (Eugene: Jordan Schnitzer Museum of Art, University of Oregon, 2015), 28.

26. Knapp, "My Life Is Work," 18.

27. Becker, "Visionary Art," 5.

28. Gerald Vizenor, *Blue Ravens* (Middletown CT: Wesleyan University Press, 2014).

29. John Adair and Sol Worth, *Through Navajo Eyes* (Bloomington: Indiana University Press, 1972) 3, 7.

30. Adair and Worth, *Through Navajo Eyes*, 255.

31. Adair and Worth, *Through Navajo Eyes*, 144.

32. Adair and Worth, *Through Navajo Eyes*, 144, 209.

8. Native *Nouveau Roman*

1. Gerald Vizenor, ed., *Survivance: Narratives of Native Presence* (Lincoln: University of Nebraska Press, 2008), 1.

2. Gerald Vizenor, *Blue Ravens* (Middletown: Wesleyan University Press, 2014), 2.

3. Marc Chagall, *My Life* (Cambridge MA: De Capo Press, 1994), 38.

4. The word "Indian" is a nomination, a mistake in navigation. The Indian is a simulation, not an actual reference to real people and cultures. Several thousand native cultures and hundreds of contemporary native languages have been reduced to a single word, "Indian." My narratives use the word "native" and specify native cultures and languages.

5. Janet Berlo and Ruth Phillips, *Native North American Art* (New York: Oxford University Press, 1998), 217.

6. Nathalie Sarraute, *Tropisms* (New York: George Braziller, 1967), vi.

7. Jason Weiss, *Writing at Risk: Interviews in Parish with Uncommon Writers* (Iowa City: University of Iowa Press, 1991) 145.

8. Leon S. Roudiez, *French Fiction Revisited* (Elmwood Park IL: Dalkey Archive Press, 1991) 29.

9. Gerald Vizenor, ed., *Native Storiers: Five Selections* (Lincoln: University of Nebraska Press, 2009), 1.

10. Vizenor, *Native Storiers*, 2.

11. Vizenor, *Native Storiers*, 3, 4.

12. Vizenor, *Native Storiers*, 4.

13. Michael Dorris, "Native American Literature in an Ethnohistorical Context," *College English* 41, no. 2 (October 1979): 147–62.

14. David Treuer, *Native American Friction: A User's Manual* (Saint Paul MN: Graywolf Press, 2006), 3, 4.

15. Louis Owens, *Other Destinies: Understanding the Indian Novel* (Norman: University of Oklahoma Press, 1992), 20.

16. Paul Shepard, *The Others: How Animals Made Us Human* (Washington DC: Island Press, 1966), 90, 91.

17. John Rogers, *Red World and White: Memories of a Chippewa Boyhood* (Norman: University of Oklahoma Press, 1974), 74. First published as *A Chippewa Speaks*, 1957.

18. John Searle, "Metaphor," in *Metaphor and Thought*, ed. Andrew Ortony (New York: Cambridge University Press, 1979), 93, 105, 123.

19. N. Scott Momaday, *The Ancient Child* (New York: Doubleday, 1989) 17.

20. Leslie Marmon Silko, *Ceremony* (New York: Viking Penguin, 1977), 132, 133.

21. Louis Owens, *Other Destinies*, 184.

22. Dorothy Lee, *Freedom and Culture* (Prospect Heights IL: Waveland Press, 1959, 1987), 60, 61.

23. George Lakoff and Mark Johnson, *Metaphors We Live By* (Chicago: University of Chicago Press, 1980), 193, 229, 235.

24. Gerald Vizenor, *Fugitive Poses: Native American Indian Scenes of Absence and Presence* (Lincoln: University of Nebraska Press, 1998), 120.

25. Gerald Vizenor, *Hiroshima Bugi: Atomu 57* (Lincoln: University of Nebraska Press, 2003), 144.

26. Paul Cuffe, *Narrative of the Life and Adventures of Paul Cuffe, a Pequot Indian: During Thirty Years at Sea, and in Traveling in Foreign Lands* (Vernon: Printed by Horace N. Brill, 1839), 4, Amherst College Digital Collection, Archive and Special Collections.

27. Jace Weaver, *The Red Atlantic: American Indigenes and the Making of the Modern World, 1000–1927* (Chapel Hill: University of North Carolina Press, 2014), 89–98. Weaver fully discusses the history and biographies of the father and son Paul Cuffe. Cuffe the senior, for instance, "counted among his friends and support-

ers Benjamin Rush (a signer of the Declaration of Independence), Albert Gallatin (the U.S. Secretary of the Treasury), and William Wilberforce (a member of the British Parliament and the leading abolitionist of his day)." Cuffe in 1812 "achieved another first when he met with President James Madison at the white House, becoming the first black man so received—but not the first Native (Indian delegations had been meeting with U.S. chief executives since George Washington)."

28. Cuffe, *Narrative of the Life*, 7.

29. Herman Melville, *Redburn: His First Voyage* (New York: The Library of America, 1983) 10.

30. Herman Melville, *Typee: A Peep of Polynesian Life* (New York: The Library of America, 1982) 252, 274.

31. Melville, *Typee*, 238.

32. Vizenor, *Hiroshima Bugi*, 202.

33. Vizenor, *Hiroshima Bugi*, 205.

34. Vizenor, *Native Storiers*, 7.

9. Time Warp Provenance

1. William Grimes, "The Indian Museum's Last Stand," *New York Times Magazine*, November 27, 1988.

2. Werner Muensterberger, *Collecting: An Unruly Passion* (Princeton: Princeton University Press, 1994), 244.

3. Muensterberger, *Collecting*, 244, 245.

4. Michael Kammen, *Visual Shock: The History of Art Controversies in American Culture* (New York: Vintage Books, 2006), 164.

5. Kammen, *Visual Shock*, 165.

6. Ellen K Foppes and Robert M. Utley, "Present at the Creation: Robert M. Utley Recalls the Beginnings of the National Historic Preservation," *Pioneers of Public History* 24, no. 2 (Spring 2002): 71, 72, accessed April 6, 2018, http://tph.ucpress.edu/content/ucptph/24/2/61.full.pdf.

7. Jane Horner, "Revolving Sequential: Concepts of Time in the Art of Carl Beam" (master of arts thesis, Carleton University, Ottawa, Canada, August 2012), 40.

8. Jann L. M. Bailey, "Firebrand Artist Daphne Odjig," *Horizons* 24, no. 4 (Spring 2011): 25.

9. Bailey, "Firebrand Artist Daphne Odjig," 27.

10. Bailey, "Firebrand Artist Daphne Odjig," 27, 28.

11. Janet C. Berlo and Ruth B. Phillips, *Native North American Art* (Oxford University Press, 1998), 226.

12. David Penny, *North American Indian Art* (London: Thames and Hudson, 2004), 14.

13. Alex Jacobs, "David Bradley's Ironic and Iconic Paintings Capture Indian Country," *Indian Country Today*, April 22, 2015.

14. Margot Fortunato Galt, *Turning the Feather Around: My Life in Art* (Saint Paul: Minnesota Historical Society, 1998), 146.

15. Jane Katz, ed., *This Song Remembers: Self Portraits of Native Americans in the Arts* (Boston: Houghton Mifflin, 1980) 60.

16. Mary Abbe, "Distinguished Artist George Morrison Dies," *Minneapolis Star Tribune*, April 18, 2000.

10. Trickster Hermeneutics

1. René Girard, *The Scapegoat* (Baltimore: Johns Hopkins University Press, 1986), 84, 85.

2. George Lakoff, *Women, Fire, and Dangerous Things* (Chicago: University of Chicago Press, 1987) 268.

3. Warwick Wadlington, *The Confidence Game in American Literature* (Princeton: Princeton University Press, 1975), 15.

4. Gerald Vizenor, *Treaty Shirts: October 2034—A Familiar Treatise on the White Earth Nation* (Middletown: Wesleyan University Press, 2016).

11. Continental Liberty

1. Harvey J. Kaye, *Thomas Paine and the Promise of America* (New York: Hill and Wang, 2005), 39, 40.

2. Thomas Paine, *Agrarian Justice* (London: W. J. Sherwin, 1817), 5.

3. Chief Joseph, "An Indian's View of Indian Affairs," *North American Review*, April 1879.

4. Gerald Vizenor, *Native Liberty: Natural Reason and Cultural Survivance* (Lincoln: University of Nebraska Press, 2009), 38.

5. Vizenor, *Native Liberty*, 41, 42.

6. William W. Warren, *History of the Ojibway Nation* (Saint Paul: Minnesota Historical Society, 1885; repr., Minneapolis: Ross and Haines, 1957), 31.

7. Elias Canetti, *Notes from Hampstead: The Writer's Notebook* (New York: Farrar, Strauss and Giroux, 1998), 27.

12. Pretense of Sovereignty

1. William Lawrence, "In Defense of Indian Rights," in *Beyond the Color Line: New Perspectives on Race and Ethnicity in America*, ed. Abigail Thernstrom and Stephan Thernstrom (Stanford: Hoover Institution Press, 2002), 393.

2. Gerald Vizenor, *Native Liberty: Natural Reason and Cultural Survivance* (Lincoln: University of Nebraska Press, 2009), 39, 40.

3. Mike Mosedale, "No Reservations," cover story in *City Pages* (Minneapolis) 22, no. 2072 (June 20, 2001).

4. Mosedale, "No Reservations."

5. Mosedale, "No Reservations."

6. Lawrence, "In Defense of Indian Rights," 393.

7. Gerald Vizenor, *The Everlasting Sky: New Voices from the People Named the Chippewa* (New York: Crowell-Collier Press, 1972), 87.

8. Lawrence, "In Defense of Indian Rights," 397.

9. William Lawrence, "Do Indian Reservations Equal Apartheid?" editorial column, *Native American Press/Ojibwe News*, June 6, 2003.

10. William Lawrence, "A Warrior's Creed: Today Is a Good Day to Die," Editorial and Commentary, *Native American Press/Ojibwe News*, September 1, 2009.

11. Obituary, *Pioneer Press*, March 4, 2010.

12. Diane White, "Farewell to the *Native American Press/Ojibwe News*," *Native American Press/Ojibwe News*, September 1, 2009.